THE LITTLE BOOK OF BIG MANAGEMENT QUESTIONS

James McGrath

THE LITTLE BOOK OF BIG MANAGEMENT QUESTIONS

THE 76 MOST IMPORTANT QUESTIONS AND HOW TO ANSWER THEM

Harlow, England • London • New York • Boston • San Francisco • Toronto • Sydney • Auckland • Singapore • Hong Kong
Tokyo • Seoul • Taipei • New Delhi • Cape Town • São Paulo • Mexico City • Madrid • Amsterdam • Munich • Paris • Milan

PEARSON EDUCATION LIMITED

Edinburgh Gate
Harlow CM20 2JE
United Kingdom
Tel: +44 (0)1279 623623
Web: www.pearson.com/uk

First published 2014 (print and electronic)

© James McGrath 2014 (print and electronic)

The right of James McGrath to be identified as author of this work has been asserted by him in accordance with the Copyright, Designs and Patents Act 1988.

Pearson Education is not responsible for the content of third-party internet sites.

ISBN: 978-1-292-01360-2 (print)
      978-1-292-01362-6 (PDF)
      978-1-292-01363-3 (ePub)
      978-1-292-01361-9 (eText)

British Library Cataloguing-in-Publication Data
A catalogue record for the print edition is available from the British Library

Library of Congress Cataloging-in-Publication Data
A catalog record for the print edition is available from the Library of Congress

10 9 8 7 6 5 4 3 2 1
17 16 15 14

Text design by Design Deluxe
Cover design by Nick Redeyoff
Print edition typeset by 3
Printed in Great Britain by Henry Ling Ltd., at the Dorset Press, Dorchester, Dorset

NOTE THAT ANY PAGE CROSS-REFERENCES REFER TO THE PRINT EDITION

In memory of my mother, Bridget McGrath, and for all those teachers who made a difference, including: Miss McCreech, St Augustine's Junior and Infant School, Handsworth; Sister Etna and Mr Begley, St Chad's Secondary Modern School, Birmingham; Dr Les Franklin, University of Central England; and Dr Des Rutherford, University of Birmingham.

CONTENTS

SECTION 3 MANAGING PROJECTS 73

SECTION 4 NAVIGATING THE WIDER ORGANISATION 103

SECTION 5 WORKING WITH CUSTOMERS AND SUPPLIERS 125

SECTION 6 MANAGING OPERATIONAL PLANS AND BUDGETS 139

SECTION 7 UNDERSTANDING FINANCIAL JARGON 159

ABOUT THE AUTHOR

Dr James McGrath qualified as an accountant in 1976. For nearly 30 years he worked in both the private and public sectors as an accountant, auditor, financial controller, senior manager and management consultant. In 1998 he joined the University of Central England, where he was the course director for the MA in Education and Professional Development and taught research skills and management and leadership. He is the co-author of four previous books: *Your Education Research Project Companion*, *Your Teacher Training Handbook*, *Your Education Leadership Handbook* (all with Anthony Coles); *The Little Book of Big Management Theories* (with Bob Bates). In 2012 he took early retirement and now writes full time. This is his first solo book. He is a Fellow of the Association of Chartered Certified Accountants and has a BA (Hons) in Politics, an MA in Education and an EdD from the University of Birmingham, where his doctoral thesis was on management and leadership. He is a lifelong supporter of West Bromwich Albion, which, he says, will earn him a reduction in his sentence should he ever find himself in Purgatory.

ACKNOWLEDGEMENTS

I would like to thank Phillip Heath and Geoff Round, who read an early draft of this book and made many valuable suggestions for how it could be improved. I'd particularly like to thank Geoff for his permission to use his TRAP project model.

I'd also like to thank my publisher Eloise Cook for her support and encouragement during the writing of this book, Natasha Whelan for the care and attention she lavished on the project and Lucy Carter for always being available to help.

PUBLISHER'S ACKNOWLEDGEMENTS

We are grateful to the following for permission to reproduce copyright material:

Extract on page 10 after *The Seven Habits of Highly Effective People*, Simon & Shuster (Covey, Stephen R. 1989) reproduced with permission from Franklin Covey; Figure on page 48 adapted from *Guide to Quality Control* 2nd ed., Asian Productivity Organization (Isikawa, K. 1986) reproduced with permission.

In some instances we have been unable to trace the owners of copyright material, and we would appreciate any information that would enable us to do so.

INTRODUCTION

M any years ago I heard a story about the chief executive of a multi-billion pound organisation who was asked by an interviewer 'Do you suffer from stress?' 'No, but I'm a carrier,' he replied.

I don't know if the story is true or merely apocryphal. But it contains a deep truth about management. It's not those at the top who suffer the most stress; it's not even those at the bottom. It's the people in the middle who endure the highest stress levels – the much-maligned middle and senior managers, who are the meat in the stress sandwich. They are the ones who have to somehow reconcile the contradictory demands of staff and the board while trying do their job, build and maintain a life outside work, and avoid strangling the next person who comes into their office and says 'Have you got a minute?' Without this cadre of managers, the visions and strategic plans of the organisation would never be implemented and staff would be left to wander about aimlessly looking for direction and meaning in their work.

This book has two aims:

- To make the life of junior, middle and senior managers a little easier by providing answers to a wide range of questions that every manager faces at some time in their career.
- To help prepare those who aspire to be a manager for the work ahead.

Unfortunately, when managers run into a problem they don't always know what to do, or who to ask for advice. Sometimes they don't want to seek help, thinking that it could be seen as a sign of weakness. So they try to work it out for themselves and learn from experience. Unfortunately, this approach can take time, and while they are learning simple problems can escalate into major disasters. This book will help you to avoid such pitfalls.

Because the book addresses the problems faced by managers throughout their careers, you will undoubtably find that some entries are more relevant to you and your current situation than others. That's fine. While I would be delighted if you read the entire book, feel free to cherry-pick the questions that you find most relevant to your current needs. But keep the book handy – you never know when it might be useful.

WHAT YOU'LL FIND IN THE BOOK

The Little Book of Big Management Questions covers 76 questions that are commonly asked by managers. To help you find the answer you need, every question has been expressed in clear, simple terms. But don't be fooled by the apparent simplicity of the questions. The answers are seldom straightforward and every one of them has the capacity to cause you serious problems if you get your response wrong.

The questions are split into seven sections. You'll find advice on:

- managing yourself
- managing people
- managing projects
- navigating the wider organisation
- working with customers and suppliers
- managing operational plans and budgets
- understanding financial jargon.

A tight focus on what is pertinent and practical means that you can get an answer to even complicated questions in just a few minutes. Unlike many management books, step-by-step advice on how to implement the solution to your problem is also provided.

All entries in the first six sections follow the same four-part format:

- why the question is important
- the business thinking behind the question
- what to do
- questions to ask yourself.

Entries in Section 7, 'Understanding financial jargon', are slightly different. As a manager you need to understand what your accountant is talking about and be able to ask meaningful questions. However, it's unlikely that you will be required to apply the information (unless you are an accountant – in which case you'll already know this stuff). Therefore, these entries are for information only. The 'What to do' and 'Questions to ask yourself' sections have been omitted, except for Question 76, which reverts to the four-part format and provides advice on how to increase profits.

There are, of course, links and overlaps between questions. To help you recognise these, each question is numbered and I use this to reference other questions that deal with different aspects of the same problem. For example, if you're reading Question 4 you might want to follow up my suggestion to *see Question* 20, which also deals with saving time.

WHAT THE BOOK CAN DO FOR YOU

If you are serious about becoming a more effective manager and you are willing to read, reflect upon and try out the advice, then this book will:

- help you to deal with a wide range of problems that every manager faces during their career;
- provide you with new ways of thinking about your relationship with staff, colleagues, key members of your organisation, customers, suppliers and other stakeholders;
- make you a better manager by improving your ability to get things done, especially the important stuff;
- help you motivate staff;
- improve your understanding of planning and accounting;
- improve your understanding of the environment in which your organisation operates;
- prepare you for promotion, and increase your personal capital and earning power.

But to get these benefits you'll need to work at it.

AND FINALLY …

As you read this book and go about your daily business of trying to fit twelve hours' work into eight, it's worth considering what Confucius said:

There were four things that the Master refused to have anything to do with: he refused to entertain conjecture or insist on certainty; he refused to be inflexible or to be egotistical.
Confucius, *Analects* 9.4

Follow the Master's advice and you won't go far wrong.
    Finally, I'd like to wish you every success in your career.

James McGrath
May 2014

HOW TO GET THE MOST OUT OF THIS BOOK

I believe that you will find the answers to many of your problems in the following pages and be able to implement the advice given fairly easily. However, you may disagree with some of the answers or feel that you can only use part of an answer in your unique circumstances. The approach suggested may not suit your personality or the organisational culture in which you operate. That's fine – there is always more than one way to solve any problem. Anyone who says that they've considered all possible options simply hasn't. The point is that the advice given will have provoked a reaction from you, and set you thinking about alternative ways to tackle the problem and your own mindset.

When reading the book, remember:

- The content is applicable to managers who work in the production and service sectors. Both are in the business of producing 'products'. A marketing firm is selling a product just as much as a company that produces car bumpers. Therefore, the content is equally applicable to managers in both sectors. You just have to ask yourself, 'How does this advice relate to my business and its processes?' and tweak the information given to your unique situation.

- The content is applicable to managers who buy or sell products externally or internally. Why should there be a difference in the standard of service provided to external customers or expected from external suppliers compared to their internal counterparts? Surely, you should aim to establish the same professional and friendly relationship with both.

- Just because the content is divided into seven sections doesn't mean that the information that is recorded in, say, Section 2 'Managing staff' can't be applied in a different context, for example when 'Managing a project' (Section 3), or vice versa.

I recommend that you keep a reflective diary in which you *very briefly* record the significant problems that you find yourself dealing with, what you did to resolve them and the results that flowed from your actions. Of course, this may not be possible, as you are almost certainly 'time starved'. If that's the case, take a few minutes on your commute home to reflect on the day's events.

Use your diary or reflection as a means of analysing both your successes and failures. Try to understand why one course of action went well and another badly, and how you might act differently if you are faced with the same or similar problem again. Learn from both your successes and failures. There is nothing shameful in failure. The great Jimmy Greaves maintains that a top-class striker converts one in every four goal-scoring opportunities they get. This means that they fail 75 per cent of the time. But they know that this failure is the price they pay for eventual success. You need to develop the same mindset.

By reflecting on what you did, you will be storing information in your subconscious. This unconscious knowledge, which I call tacit knowledge (*see Question 5*), and John Adair refers to as deep knowledge, is what an older generation called gut instinct. It's knowledge that you don't even know you have but which informs your thinking and actions on a daily basis. For example, have you ever been struggling with a problem or decision for hours when suddenly out of the blue a resolution just popped into your mind? Fully formed and quite possibly totally different to anything you'd previously considered? That's your tacit knowledge at work.

SECTION 1

MANAGING YOURSELF

A gentleman who studies is unlikely to be inflexible. Make it your guiding principle to do your best for others and to be trustworthy in what you say … When you make a mistake do not be afraid of mending your ways.

Confucius, *Analects* 1.8

INTRODUCTION

This section is about you and your management attitudes, knowledge and skills. Before you can manage other people effectively, you need to be aware of your own strengths and weaknesses. Use this section to identify where you are already strong and those areas where further work is required. Only then can you build on your strengths and find ways to compensate for your weaknesses. Remember, no manager is perfect. There is always further work to be done if you want to become the best manager you can be.

If it's not already obvious from the quote at the start of this section, you need to be flexible in how you deal with problems that arise and willing to admit when you were wrong. Only then will you be free to try another approach. If you find that your strategy isn't working, don't fall into the trap of thinking it's the people you're working with who are causing the problem. Always remember that one definition of madness is doing the same thing over and over again in the expectation of a different result.

Confucius also refers to trustworthiness. As a manager, your most important asset is your reputation. People respect and follow those who they trust. So when things go wrong, don't blame some poor person who works for you. Accept that, as the person in charge, you are ultimately responsible for both your own actions and those of your staff. If you can combine this with never stealing someone else's idea or work and passing it off as your own, staff will respect and trust you. Such feelings create a strong and powerful foundation upon which to build a relationship with staff and colleagues.

QUESTION 1 WHAT'S MY MANAGEMENT STYLE?

Why it's important: Every manager has a default management style. You need to know what yours is so that you can consciously vary it when circumstances require a different approach.

Douglas McGregor, who revolutionised management thinking when he wrote *The Human Side of Enterprise*, identified two sets of beliefs that managers have about staff. As with all stereotypes, the two descriptions do not reflect the reality of most managers' views, which usually reside somewhere in the middle.

THEORY X MANAGERS BELIEVE THAT:

People are lazy, untrustworthy, dislike work and will try to avoid it if possible.

People want a quiet life and shun responsibility, lack ambition and want job security above all else.

To make people work, a manager has to constantly monitor their actions and threaten them with sanctions.

THEORY Y MANAGERS BELIEVE THAT:

People are naturally creative, imaginative and enjoy the challenges that work brings.

People are self-motivated, want to do a good job and actively seek responsibility and the opportunity to stretch themselves.

The best thing a manager can do is provide the conditions that enable people to flourish, and give them as much autonomy as possible.

Because of their beliefs, Theory X managers adopt a command and control approach to management.

In contrast, Theory Y managers do not seek to control their staff. They give them the autonomy to exercise their discretion. However, they retain the right to tell staff what to do.

WHAT TO DO

- Reread the above descriptions again. Give each description a percentage score to indicate your level of agreement with each statement. Your two scores must equal 100 per cent. There is no correct answer, so give the first figure that pops into your head.

- If you prefer a Theory X approach, you allow staff very little autonomy, seldom use delegation and require staff to refer most decisions to you. This will create more work for you. Do you want this?

- If you prefer Theory Y, you use delegation extensively and expect staff only to refer issues back to you when there is a problem. This is fine with good people, but what about staff who are unreliable?

- Remember that it's very difficult to change your view of humanity. But if you know your default management style you can consciously decide to change it when circumstances demand. For example, if you're a Theory X manager you might delegate more to 'trusted people'. If you're a Theory Y manager then in a crisis you may become more controlling.

- Extreme changes in behaviour of any kind are usually counterproductive, as staff trust people who are consistent and distrust those whose behaviour is unpredictable. Therefore, whether you are an X or Y manager, use the following approach. Establish clear rules for all the important/essential areas of work; for example, the level of performance required, meeting deadlines, the need to follow procedures, individual levels of autonomy and standards of behaviour. Always uphold and enforce these basic rules.

- Having established a level of control over your team's essential activities, try to be more relaxed with the other stuff. The modern business world is too complex and fast moving for any one person to have all the answers. A more relaxed approach will enable you to use your staff's knowledge, imagination and insights to improve your team's performance and your own.

QUESTIONS TO ASK YOURSELF

- What event/events influenced the adoption of my default management stance?

- What changes can I make to my management style that will improve productivity and my relations with staff?

QUESTION 2   DO I MANAGE OR LEAD PEOPLE?

Why it's important: Increasingly organisations are looking for managers with leadership skills/potential – especially when looking to fill senior positions and board vacancies.

The reality is that in every organisation managers are required to lead and leaders are required to manage. But if you spend all your time on the management activities (see column one in the table below) you will be perceived as a manager. To be seen as a leader, or someone with leadership potential, you need to get stuck into the activities in column two.

Managers are concerned with:	Leaders are concerned with:
The present	The future
Plans	Vision
Maintenance of systems	The big picture
Maintaining the status quo	Change
Feedback	Inspiration
Objectives	Outcomes
Monitoring and controlling staff	Exercising influence over followers
Providing a sense of order	Providing a sense of purpose and direction for followers
Spreading organisational culture	Building organisational culture
Doing things right	Doing the right things
Dealing with complexity within and around the organisation	Dealing with change and the effects of change
Producing order and consistency	Producing change and movement
Planning and budgeting	Vision building and strategising
Organisational structure and staffing	Aligning people behind a common vision or set of objectives
Problem solving	Problem identification in advance and eradication at source
Economy and efficiency	Effectiveness
Staying on the right path	Making new paths

Source: J. McGrath, 'Leading in a Managerialist Paradigm: A Survey of Perceptions within a Faculty of Education', doctoral thesis, University of Birmingham, 2004.

WHAT TO DO

■ From memory, list the tasks you've performed over the past week. Include meetings, interactions with staff and both routine and one-off jobs.

■ Analyse what you've been up to and summarise similar activities under a single heading, for example instructing staff, problem solving, etc. Calculate how much time you spent under each heading.

■ Use the table above to allocate each task to either a management or leadership heading. Don't worry if most of your work is categorised as management.

■ Use your new knowledge to reorient your thinking from that of a manager to that of a leader. For example, instead of solving single problems, consider if they are symptoms of a widespread problem and eliminate the causes at source (see Question 20).

■ Stop being parochial. Develop what the management guru Charles Handy calls the helicopter approach. Rise above your professional and departmental concerns and view problems in organisational terms – and select the solution that is in the best interest of the entire organisation. If you can see 'the big picture' it will mark you out as executive material.

■ Continue to deal with day-to-day issues (see Question 17) but also spend time considering the future threats (see Question 48) and opportunities that face your team, and address them before they arrive at your door.

■ Stop emphasising processes and concentrate instead on improving outcomes by providing staff with a bit of inspiration. Remember, actions speak louder than words, so lead by example.

■ Repeat your audit every eight weeks until you achieve a satisfactory balance between management and leadership.

■ Remember, the higher you climb, the more you will be expected to provide leadership as well as manage your operation.

QUESTIONS TO ASK YOURSELF

■ Do I want to be a leader or am I happy being a manager?

■ Do I need to learn more about leadership and develop my leadership skills?

QUESTION 3 WHAT POWER DO I HAVE AND HOW CAN I USE IT?

Why it's important: Management is difficult. To succeed you must use all the tools at your disposal. Power and authority are two of your most effective tools – if used correctly.

Between them, Max Weber, Charles Handy and John French and Bertram Raven identified seven types of power/authority.

SEVEN SOURCES OF POWER:

Traditional authority is power that is bequeathed from one generation to another; although it is most obvious in rich/royal families it can also exist within elite groups.

Legal rational authority gives a post holder the right to exercise all the powers of that office and to expect people to follow their instructions.

Charismatic power or charisma is an innate personal characteristic that enables the holder to attract people to them by the force of their personality, beliefs and/or actions.

Reward power is based on the leader's ability to grant or withhold financial and non-financial rewards.

Coercive power is based on the leader's ability to impose sanctions or punishments on followers.

Expert power is available to both managers and staff and relates to a person's recognised expertise in a specific area of work.

Negative power can be utilised by both managers and staff and is the ability to throw a spanner in the works and disrupt, block or stop things happening.

Develop and use as many sources of power as you can. This is important because, like chess pieces, when you combine two or more sources/pieces then synergy occurs: a case of $2 + 2 = 5$.

WHAT TO DO

- Many managers feel uncomfortable telling people what to do. Get over it. Power is an essential management tool. So use it.

■ Examine the seven sources of power above and use the table below to record the level of power you currently exercise. Use the bullet points after the table to identify how you are going to increase your power under each heading.

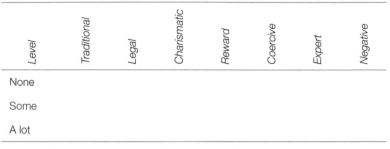

Level	Traditional	Legal	Charismatic	Reward	Coercive	Expert	Negative
None							
Some							
A lot							

■ Confirm the limits of any traditional or positional authority you have. When you issue an instruction, expect compliance and don't let anyone ignore your instruction.

■ Identify the financial and non-financial rewards you can offer. Find out what motivates each member of staff and use that knowledge to make the most appropriate offer (*see Question 21*).

■ Identify how much coercive power you really have. Can you sack, suspend, demote or withdraw an individual's privileges? But remember, coercive actions create ill will and should be used sparingly.

■ Identify what expert power you have and exploit it. If you have little or no expert power, develop an expertise in an area useful to the organisation.

■ Don't assume you have no charismatic power. Like beauty, charisma is in the eye of the beholder. Act with integrity, model the behaviour you expect from staff, and be fair and honest in all your dealings and you'll be surprised how people will view you.

■ Use negative power sparingly. It may work, but if you block or derail someone's pet initiative there may be a price to pay. Remember that staff can also exercise negative power against you.

■ Implement the above advice and then complete the above table again in about eight weeks to see how far you've progressed.

QUESTIONS TO ASK YOURSELF

■ Do I worry about telling people what to do? If so, why?

■ What can I do to remove such worries? Do I need assertiveness training?

QUESTION 4 HOW CAN I WORK SMARTER, NOT HARDER, AND BECOME MORE PRODUCTIVE?

Why it's important: The one thing that all managers lack is time. To become more productive, you have to guard against time thieves.

If you want to be recognised as a manager with a future you have to stand out from the crowd. One way to do this is to deliver results above what is expected of you. Stephen Covey's time management matrix can help you free up time, which you can then spend on the important stuff.

COVEY ANALYSED WHAT MANAGERS DO IN FOUR CATEGORIES:

Urgent and important: Crises that blow up quickly, demands from on high and the need to meet urgent deadlines.

Not urgent but important: Jobs that if completed would save you time in the future by resolving problems at source rather than continually dealing with the symptoms of the problem. Unfortunately they usually take a backseat to the urgent stuff.

Not urgent and not important: Interruptions caused by phone calls, visits and emails dealing with social issues or problems that don't affect you or your team.

Urgent but not important: Other people's crises that they try to make yours.

Source: After *The Seven Habits of Highly Effective People*, Simon & Schuster (Covey, Stephen R. 1989) reproduced with permission from Franklin Covey.

If you have the self-discipline and assertiveness required, you can use Covey's model to save you time, which you can then invest in projects that will increase your productivity and get you noticed.

WHAT TO DO

- Ditch your 'to do' lists.
- Record how you spend your time over a week. At the end of the week, analyse your activities using Covey's four descriptors.
- Urgent and important tasks are probably the issues you currently spend most time on. They need to be dealt with quickly, since in many cases they will help you achieve your targets.
- Not urgent but important are the tasks languishing in your drawer. To resolve these, follow the example of the best manager I came across in my 45-year career. He would arrive at work at 6.00 am every day. Seldom did his phone ring before 9.00 am. He used this quiet time to deal with the important but not urgent stuff. Working in the morning is more productive than at night as you will be fresher and there will be fewer people around to distract you. If you follow this approach and invest a little time up front you'll reduce the number of urgent problems you have to deal with, as you will have eliminated their cause at source (*see Question 20*).
- With not urgent and not important tasks, stop them landing on your desk in the first place by explaining to the 'sender' that they need to speak to X. If they get through your 'firewall', bin them or delegate them if they require action.
- The urgent but not important category is filled with other people's issues. Don't allow other people to dump their problems on you (unless it's your boss). Be a good colleague but make sure that their work is slotted into your priorities. Be assertive and don't allow people to steal your time.

QUESTIONS TO ASK YOURSELF

- Which of the not urgent but important jobs in my in-tray would save me most time or resolve the most recurring problems?
- Which tasks should I redirect at source to another member of staff?

QUESTION 5   IS IT EVER OK TO RELY ON GUT INSTINCT?

Why it's important: Eighty per cent of what you know about your job is held in the form of tacit knowledge.

The last 30 years has seen a greater emphasis on scientific approaches to management. This has made some people wary of making decisions based on gut instinct. Instead they try to evaluate every issue using various quantitative techniques. This is a mistake (*see Question 75*).

Friedrich von Hayek won the Nobel Prize for economics for his work on free market economics. One reason he supported free markets was because devolved staff find it impossible to report to the centre everything they know about local conditions, problems and opportunities. This is because much of what they know is held in the form of tacit knowledge or what John Adair calls deep knowledge. This knowledge resides in their subconscious but informs their thinking and actions on a daily basis without them being aware of it.

There are thousands of examples of such tacit knowledge at work – for example, when a new manager makes an entirely logical suggestion about how to reorganise a process but those involved in it know instinctively that it will never work for reasons they can't fully explain.

So the simple answer to 'Can I rely on my gut instincts?' is yes.

WHAT TO DO

■ Remember that storing information is the key to tacit knowledge.

■ Use every opportunity to gather information about your organisation from staff, managers, customer, suppliers and wider stakeholders.

■ Walk the job and talk to everyone from the office cleaner to the chair of the company, and everyone in between. (A cleaner once told me in advance of a board meeting that the firm's sales were predicted to decline over the next six months. She'd seen the returns on the sales manager's desk that morning.)

■ Use meetings and the general chit-chat that goes on before and after them as an opportunity to add to your knowledge.

■ Use observation at meetings to learn about the people present, including their attitudes, beliefs, motives and relationship with colleagues.

■ Read any reports that appear in the press or on the web about your organisation.

■ Be on the lookout for bits of information and ideas that arise when you are watching the TV, reading, talking to friends, online, etc. Anything that strikes you as interesting and that might have a bearing on your work is worth storing away. Our unconscious mind uses these disparate and unconnected pieces of data, in a process of synthesis, to produce new ideas and theories.

■ Always be on the lookout for clever ideas in other organisations that you can import and adapt to use in your own.

■ If you keep a reflective diary, jot down any interesting comments, events, trends, problems, opportunities, threats or juicy gossip (even knowing who's sleeping with whom can be valuable if it explains someone's attitude/stance).

■ All the above information will compost down in your subconscious and form linkages and connections in your brain, which will enrich your tacit knowledge. When faced with a problem this knowledge will resurface and provide you with an answer.

QUESTIONS TO ASK YOURSELF

■ Can I identify an occasion when I was faced with a problem and I just knew what the right course of action was?

■ How good am I at collecting and using information about my organisation and the people in it?

QUESTION 6   HOW CAN I BECOME BETTER AT RECEIVING NEGATIVE FEEDBACK?

Why it's important: Nobody likes to be criticised but it is only by listening to criticism and acting upon what's been said that we can improve our performance.

While you should be always willing to fight your own corner, especially when undeserved criticism or blame is directed at you, you must learn to accept and use negative feedback. Why? For the simple reason that there are aspects of our character that are unknown to us. According to the psychologists Joseph Luft and Harry Ingram, everyone has four areas to their personality, with the contents of two areas remaining hidden from the person. Their Johari windows model consists of four window panes of different sizes. The different sizes of window are intended to show how very different quantities of information reside in each pane.

- **Open arena**: Aspects known to the individual and others.
- **Hidden façade**: Aspects known to the individual but not others.
- **Blind spot**: Aspects known to others but not to the individual.
- **Unknown**: Aspects not known to the individual or others.

Good feedback can help you identify and deal with those aspects of your character that reside in your blind spot. Alas, you may never know what resides in your unknown area.

WHAT TO DO

- If feedback is to be given after observation of a specific event, identify in advance the criteria the appraiser is going to use to assess your performance. If there are no criteria, think about what criteria you would use. Keep these criteria in mind when preparing for the appraisal event.
- Insist that the feedback is given to you in private and that sufficient time is allowed.
- Take notes of what is said by the appraiser.
- Remember that the appraiser giving feedback is not criticising you, they are criticising your actions. Your actions are not you, so don't take anything said personally.
- Disengage your competitive streak and say nothing. Don't think about what you are going to say when the person stops talking. Just listen to what is being said.
- Don't argue with the appraiser or try to justify your actions. Just listen and absorb what's being said.
- Don't become emotional or make an emotional appeal to the appraiser to understand the situation you were in. Concentrate instead on what they say.
- Don't try to change the subject or blame other people for your actions.
- Don't dismiss what you're told because you think the appraiser doesn't like you or they are out to get you.
- Do ask questions about anything you don't understand or which you would like clarified.
- If possible, try to put the feedback out of your mind for 24 hours. Only then sit down and review your notes and what was said.
- Keep your emotions out of your analysis. Identify the key points made by the appraiser. Consider how you might have dealt differently with each of these issues.
- If you have the time, record what you have learnt in your reflective diary and use that information when faced with a similar issue.

QUESTIONS TO ASK YOURSELF

- Are there any issues that, if raised, might cause me to react negatively?
- How have I usually reacted to negative feedback? Was this effective/ appropriate?

QUESTION 7 LOOKING AT WHAT I DO, WHICH STUFF ADDS THE MOST VALUE?

Why it's important: Managers are judged on results, and the direct or indirect impact that they make to the organisation's bottom line.

Some organisations make it very clear to managers what their priorities are. Others don't. This question is aimed at those managers who receive limited direction from their board or bosses.

If you are selling goods or services to an external customer, you can easily identify which products contribute most to the bottom line. If your customers are other departments within the organisation, and you don't operate as a trading centre (*see Question 68*), it's a lot more difficult.

Managers are human and they have preferences, which can colour their view as to which tasks they think generate the most value. To counter this bias, talk to your internal customers and boss and collect data on which activities they think add most value.

Once you have collected some data, use the Pareto principle to identify the 20 per cent of your outputs that produce 80 per cent of the total value of your outputs. The Pareto principle, or the theory of the important few and unimportant many, was developed by economist Vilfredo Pareto. For over 80 years it has been applied in many situations. For example, 80 per cent of an organisation's profits will be earned by 20 per cent of its products, while 80 per cent of the organisation's income will be derived from 20 per cent of its customers.

Knowing about the Pareto principle doesn't solve your problems but it does enable you, along with using the other data you collected, to identify which tasks generate the most value.

WHAT TO DO

- Identify what outputs you and your team have produced over the last month. These could be products sold to a customer or reports issued to management. Either way, they are outputs.

- Collect financial and non-financial data to assess the value of the outputs you produce. Some outputs may have very little direct financial impact but that doesn't mean that their indirect impact on decision making or planning should be undermined (*see Question 75*).

- If a product or service is sold externally, you should find it fairly easy to discover how much it contributes to the bottom line by having a chat with your sales manager or accountant.

- If a product or service is 'sold' internally, find out what value the recipient of the product or service places on it. The best way to do this is to chat with your internal customers and ask them: 'What do you use it for?'; 'How useful is It?'; 'Does the product meet your requirements?'; 'How could it be improved?' What you are looking for are the products or services that have the greatest impact on the organisation in terms of increases in economy, efficiency, effectiveness (*see Question 65*) or profits.

- If all your outputs can be measured in monetary terms then ranking is simple and the most valuable outputs can be quickly identified. However, if you are relying on non-financial data, score each output you produce as 1 (low), 2 (medium), 3 (high), 4 (very high) and 5 (essential), using the qualitative information you've collected from your internal customers/boss.

- Use your scored list to identify the 20 per cent of outputs that generates 80 per cent of the value.

- It is this 20 per cent of products or services that you need to safeguard. They are your priority outputs – whatever you do, don't let standards slip or delays occur in their production.

QUESTIONS TO ASK YOURSELF

- Who are my customers?
- How much do I know about what my customers want and/or need?

QUESTION 8

HOW CAN I MANAGE MY BOSS AND GET AWAY WITH IT?

Why it's important: Your success in any organisation is largely dependent on your relationship with your boss.

The relationship you have with your boss is vital to your success and career prospects. A good relationship can form the basis of a hugely effective and enjoyable partnership for both parties. A poor relationship means you become involved in either a cold – or sometimes a hot – war with someone who has more power than you and who is always going to win.

Managing your boss isn't about manipulating them. It's about establishing a mutually beneficial relationship based upon trust, need and respect. You'll notice that I haven't included friendship or liking in the list. It's great if aspects of these do exist, but the relationship with your boss is primarily a professional one.

Your aim is to accumulate a certain amount of goodwill and influence with your boss, which you can call upon when required.

WHAT TO DO

- To manage your boss, you have to know how they do things, what they like, dislike and value. Then you can adapt your approach accordingly.
- Don't monopolise your manager's time. You're not the only person they manage. Keep meetings short and productive. If you need to send them a 30-page report, summarise the main points in one or two pages. Never provide them with just raw data. It's your job to analyse and evaluate the data and report results as useful information.
- Your boss has enough problems already – don't add to them by becoming one of the 20 per cent of staff that cause 80 per cent of their problems (*see Question 7*).
- A good relationship is built on trust. Your manager must be able to trust you when you say 'I'll get it done by Monday', and trust the quality of your work – especially when they have to sign it off.
- Bosses have enough problems, so when you take a problem to them be armed with a range of solutions and/or partial solutions.

- Always show loyalty. Don't speak critically of your boss to staff or other managers. If you do, they'll hear about it because it will benefit someone to tell them. Be frank and honest at all times and never mislead or lie to them.

- Don't disagree with your boss in public. If you have concerns over an issue, raise it in private. Often you will find that their decision was influenced by information you were unaware of.

- Become invaluable to your boss. Identify the areas of work they dislike or lack expertise in and provide expert support in these areas (*see Question 3*).

- Do the above and you will create a professional relationship based on mutual trust and professional respect. This is the ideal basis upon which to enter into negotiations with your boss about what you should be doing and what your targets and priorities should be (*see Question 29*), and avoiding a situation in which your boss imposes their decisions on you.

QUESTIONS TO ASK YOURSELF

- What expert knowledge do I have or could develop that my boss would find useful?

- Do I understand fully what my boss expects of me?

QUESTION 9 HOW DO I DELIVER A REALLY EFFECTIVE PRESENTATION?

Why it's important: Increasingly managers are required to make presentations to their staff and other managers. Presentations are also becoming common components of many job interviews.

For some reason the thought of speaking in public terrifies many managers. I've known some excellent managers who would rather go swimming naked in a shoal of jellyfish than make a presentation. Yet if ever there was an instance of good planning preventing poor performance then presentations are it.

Prepare well and any presentation is a doddle. Why? Because the focus of a presentation is the presenter and their views, beliefs or opinions. It is the presenter who determines the structure and content of the presentation and determines when and how questions will be taken, if at all. Such control is seldom available to a manager in normal day-to-day work.

WHAT TO DO

- Identify the aims and purpose of the presentation. Write these down and refer to them constantly during your planning and preparation.

- Research your prospective audience: who will be there, how many, what do they know about the topic of the presentation, etc. Use this information to determine at what level you'll pitch the presentation. But always remember the anagram KISS (keep it simple stupid).

- The time you have for the presentation will determine both its structure and content. Avoid too much detail. Presentations are concerned with providing an overview of key points, not exploring the minutiae of an issue. Include the detailed stuff in any handout you prepare.

- Think of your presentation as a three-act play. In the first act (introduction) set the scene and outline the content of the presentation. The second act is the main body of your presentation. Then in the third act (conclusion) summarise for the audience what you've said.

- Never start a presentation with a joke. If it falls flat, you'll feel terrible. Any humour used should arise naturally from the subject matter or interaction with the audience.

■ During the introduction say that you will take questions at the end. That way you can control the time you leave for questions.

■ If possible, practise your presentation in front of an audience. But if even your loved ones don't want to listen, practise in front of a mirror. Always time yourself.

■ Don't overrun.

■ Speak clearly. Don't mumble, but show enthusiasm for what you're saying. Slow your delivery down by about 10 per cent compared to how you speak normally. Vary your pitch and tone, and sound interested and enthusiastic. To emphasise a point, pause briefly after you have finished talking about it.

■ People are tired of the standard PowerPoint presentations. To make your presentation interesting, use photos, clips from the internet or solid objects such as pieces of machinery instead of the ubiquitous PowerPoint slides.

■ If you need specific equipment, such as a projector, make sure in advance that it's available and working. Plan for possible equipment failure by having a fall-back position.

■ Never read from a script. Either use brief notes as an aide-memoire, or better still your PowerPoint slides or props as a prompt for what you want to say.

■ Make regular eye contact with your audience and check their body language and facial expressions. If they look lost or confused at any stage, rephrase and repeat what you think they didn't understand.

■ At the end, thank your audience and ask for any questions.

QUESTIONS TO ASK YOURSELF

■ Which aspects of a presentation am I good/bad at?

■ Would I benefit from further training on presentations or should I just get more experience under my belt?

QUESTION 10　HOW CAN I MAKE MEETINGS MORE PRODUCTIVE?

Why it's important: If you call a one-hour meeting and six staff attend, that's seven hours' work that didn't get done. You need to make sure it was worth the trade-off.

Meetings are the bane of modern business life. We all complain about them but then get annoyed if we're excluded from a meeting that we think we should have been at. It's likely that you will have to attend a lot of meetings chaired by colleagues or senior managers. There's not much you can do about how they are managed – other than avoiding the worst time-wasting events if possible. But there are plenty of improvements you can make to your own meetings.

WHAT TO DO

- Only hold a meeting if it's absolutely necessary.
- Avoid establishing routine weekly or monthly meetings. Too often they become a regular event that people feel obliged to attend.
- Always identify the purpose of the meeting in advance and only invite those people who are involved with or affected by the issue on the agenda.
- Advertise the start and finish time of the meeting. Start on time, even if some people are missing. They'll soon get the message. And finish when you said you would. No exceptions. People will quickly tailor their inputs to the meeting to fit in with such a regime.
- Keep the agenda short and focused and specify how long each item will be discussed for. Enforce the cut-off ruthlessly, even if further discussion is required. The discussion can then continue at the next meeting (which might be held immediately following the end of the current meeting if it's vitally important). Again, what you are doing is sending a message to the participants that the timescales will be adhered to without exception.
- Chair the meeting yourself and don't allow digressions or let people raise new issues/problems. Tell them to table the items for the next meeting.
- Don't keep minutes of the meeting. Instead, maintain a list of action

points that have been agreed during the meeting. Immediately after the meeting email a list of the action points to all attendees, with details of who is responsible for each action and a deadline completion date.

■ Monitor completion of all action points and hold individuals to account when they fail to deliver on time (*see Question 29*).

■ Don't serve tea or coffee and never biscuits. It will only turn part of the meeting into an unofficial tea break and an opportunity to discuss the football, who's favourite to get the new sales job and 'Have you heard about X in the design department'?

■ If you have the nerve, consider holding all your meetings standing up. You'll be amazed at how quickly you get through the agenda.

QUESTIONS TO ASK YOURSELF

■ How many regular meetings do I currently attend per month? How many of them can I eliminate?

■ Do I have the right people attending my meetings? When was the last time I reviewed the list of attendees?

QUESTION 11 HOW CAN I GET EVERYONE TO CONTRIBUTE/SPEAK AT MEETINGS?

Why it's important: Meetings are supposed to improve decision making or outcomes by pooling the knowledge of those present. If someone fails to speak, they add nothing to the meeting.

I'm sure you've attended many meetings where a significant proportion of those present said nothing. Such people fall into two groups. For those in Group A the meeting is of no interest whatsoever and they only attend out of habit or because they were told to. They use the meeting as a convenient place to rest up or plan their weekend away with Richard or Claire in accounts. Those in Group B may well have something to contribute to the meeting but feel constrained from expressing their views and ideas because of lack of confidence or embarrassment.

Whatever the reason for people's silence, you need to deal with it. Time is too precious for a member of staff to waste time fantasising about their next away day. And shyness can't be allowed to stymie the flow of fresh new ideas from junior members of staff or those who are chronically shy.

WHAT TO DO

- Implement the suggestions outlined in Question 10. This will alert your team to the fact that you are committed to making meetings more effective.

- Identify which people have no interest in the meeting and have a chat with them. Suggest that their time and expertise is too valuable to waste in meaningless meetings and tell them that their presence will no longer be required. Make it clear that if anything that relates specifically to their area of work comes up, you'll call them in.

- Chat to those who you think are too shy/diffident to speak at meetings. Explain how their unique viewpoint could be of real value by offering an insight into problems from their perspective/position in the team. This is not a load of bull in the guise of reassurance. Often it is the most junior members of a team who see the problem most clearly as they are at the sharp end (*see Question 53*).

- Don't let the more self-assured or senior staff intimidate junior staff. Make it clear that you want to hear everyone's opinion.

- During meetings let those who wish to express a view do so. But monitor the time and cut short digressions and rambling expositions. Once all the 'volunteers' have spoken, canvass the views of those who have said nothing on the issue. Don't embarrass them. Simply ask 'How do you feel about this?' or 'Have you anything you'd like to add to what's been said?' Do this a few times and even the shyest person will realise that it's better to offer their opinion in the flow of the discussion than wait for you to question them in full view of the group.

- After the meeting, take the time to speak to the people individually who've started to open up. Thank them for their contribution and encourage them to speak more often.

- Whenever a good idea is suggested, welcome it and make sure that the person responsible gets the credit for it.

QUESTIONS TO ASK YOURSELF

- Do I monopolise the meeting and stop others from speaking?
- What's the culture of the meeting? Is it supportive or competitive? Do I need to change it?

QUESTION 12 HOW CAN I DELEGATE EFFECTIVELY?

Why it's important: You don't have the time to do everything yourself. To be effective you have to delegate.

Many managers worry about delegating work. They don't want to be seen as dumping work on people, which can make those people resentful. In some instances they don't trust their staff (*see Question 1*) to do a good job. Others don't want to relinquish control over the work. While yet others think it's quicker to do the work themselves.

The situational leadership theory of Ken Blanchard and Paul Hersey provides an excellent guide to how delegation can be managed. They suggest that when giving someone a task to do it's essential to identify the level of direction and support they need. Direction relates to the amount of guidance you give the person on how to do the actual job – the technical stuff. Support relates to the amount of reassurance you provide; for example, if the person lacks self-confidence in their ability to do the job, you provide the reassurance that they need to complete the job.

By combining the level of direction and support, four strategies arise.

FOUR APPROACHES TO DELEGATION:

Coaching: High direction and high support is provided to those who you think lack technical knowledge on how to do the work and have little self-belief.

Directing: High direction and low support is provided to those who you think are self-confident but lack experience of the work.

Supporting: High support and low direction is provided to those who you believe are very capable of doing the work but lack self-belief or worry about doing something for the first time.

Delegating: Low support and low direction is provided to those who you know have high levels of technical skills and are self-confident and assured.

WHAT TO DO

- Remember that the better you know and understand your staff, the more effective you will be in selecting the right person to delegate each job to (*see Question 21*).

- Select who you think is the most suitable person to do the job. Brief them about what needs to be done and get a feel for how they see the job. Ask questions such as 'What are you going to do first?' or 'Is there anything that worries you about what I've asked you to do?'

- Based on your discussion, select the model of delegation you think is most appropriate: coaching, directing, supporting or delegating.

- Set a deadline for the completion of the work and specify a set of criteria that the work has to meet (*see Question 29*).

- If the work is going to be completed over an extended period of time, book an early review meeting to check progress. Based on the results of that meeting, decide if further meetings are required.

- Reassure the person that if they run into problems they can see you at any time and don't have to wait for an arranged meeting.

- Don't fall into the trap of thinking that people move through the four approaches outlined in a straight line. Every time you give a person a new job/task, you have to identify anew which approach to use with them because they have not done that task before.

- Of course, delegation is always much easier if you recruited good people in the first place (*see Question 16*), trained them well, and encouraged them to stretch and challenge themselves.

QUESTIONS TO ASK YOURSELF

- Do I delegate enough? What stops me from delegating more?

- Do I always brief staff fully and provide criteria to assess the quality of the work?

QUESTION 13 HOW DO I MAKE BETTER DECISIONS?

Why it's important: Ultimately the quality of your decision making will determine how successful you are as a manager.

The standard approach to decision making involves an eight-stage process:

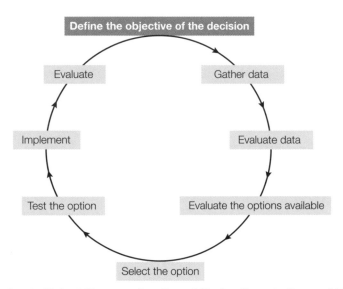

According to Robert Townsend, author of *Up the Organization* and *Further Up the Organization* and former director of Avis Cars, it is important to understand the key elements to decision making:

UNDERSTANDING DECISIONS:

Decisions should be made at the lowest level possible in the organisation.

There are only two types of decision: those that can be made quickly because they are cheap and easy to correct, and those that should only be taken after careful consideration because they are expensive and difficult to correct.

All decisions are made on the basis of incomplete data.

A good manager gets one-third of their decisions right and one-third wrong. The other one-third would have turned out just as it did whatever decision was made.

WHAT TO DO

■ Don't get hung up over decisions. Delaying a decision or not making a decision are decisions in their own right and have consequences.

■ Don't pass decisions up the line when you have the authority to make them. It will make you look indecisive.

■ Have the confidence to take decisions that are cheap and easy to correct and can be made with minimal information.

■ Delay taking decisions that are expensive and difficult to correct until you have adequate, but not complete, data. You should use both quantitative and qualitative data (*see Question 75*) and your own tacit knowledge (*see Question 5*). What constitutes adequate data will depend on the nature of the decision/project and your own risk profile.

■ Don't take into account what has already been spent when making a decision. Such money has gone for good. Look only at future cash flows. If you have already spent £4 million on a project and need to spend a further £1 million to complete it, compare that £1 million with future cash flows and not £5 million (£4 million + £1 million). If future receipts are predicted to exceed £1 million you might decide to proceed, but if they are below £1 million you fold. Never think 'We've got to get something in return for the £4 million already spent' (*see Question 69*).

■ While you can never have complete data when making a decision, you should subject the data you do have to critical evaluation. Ask if the data has been affected by: incorrect assumptions, wishful thinking, errors in calculation, overconfident projections (including customer numbers and cash flows) or an underestimation of risk.

■ Always carry out a post-decision review. If you don't, you're missing a great opportunity to identify errors in your decision-making process and improve future performance.

QUESTIONS TO ASK YOURSELF

■ What's my risk profile? Am I a risk taker or avoider?

■ How much information do I routinely require before I will make a decision: 25, 50, 75 or 90 per cent of information available?

HOW DO I PROJECT A PROFESSIONAL IMAGE?

Why it's important: Substance should always be more important than image. But in today's world people are often judged on their image alone (at least initially).

The advice here is specifically aimed at those who aspire to be a manager or who are junior managers.

In today's business world it's not sufficient to do your job if you want to be promoted. You also need to project the right professional image.

I've long thought that there are three types of managers:

Workers   Warriors

Types of managers

Wanderers

- **Workers** are not particularly bothered about advancement, because their true interests lie outside work. They want to do a good job and then go home and indulge their passion – be it amateur dramatics or fell walking. These people are the backbone of every organisation and should be valued.

- **Warriors** work hard, are ambitious and know that they have to present a professional image to the world. These people are the future of every business and need to be nurtured.

- **Wanderers** are only interested in advancing their own career. Every decision they make is based on 'What's best for me?'. They are often keen on making changes, as it bulks up their CV, but leave before the full effects of the change are known. They tend to their image as carefully as any Hollywood star. These people will look after themselves.

It's the warriors who need to get the balance right between working hard and presenting the right professional image, if they want to avoid being labelled as workers.

WHAT TO DO

- Remember that first impressions count, so how you look and present yourself is important.

- Comply with the dress code of your organisation. Choose conservative colours and ensure that the clothes fit you well and are comfortable to work in.

- Ask a friend or partner if you have any annoying habits, and then eradicate them. For example, do you end every sentence with 'OK' or 'Like', or chew your hair?

- Always appear self-confident but not arrogant – especially if you are terrified. Stand tall, smile and look people in the eye when you speak.

- Improve your communication skills. People make judgements about you based upon how you speak and write. Keep your communications simple, clear and unambiguous. Don't join the idiots who pepper everything they say with moronic management speak such as 'Let's go open kimono on this'.

- Turn out quality work. Never be happy with work that's just OK. We all have bad days, but aim to produce work at 80 per cent of your best as a minimum.

- Professional practitioners such as accountants, lawyers and doctors are expected to place their client's interest above their own. Your client is the organisation, so act accordingly.

- Establish a reputation for honesty and integrity (*see Question 15*). Once established, protect, enhance and safeguard it.

- Identify someone within your organisation who can act as a role model for how you would like to be perceived. Don't be afraid to pinch ideas from them. But remember, just as every great band copied their idols, they had to find their own style before they became great. You need to do the same.

QUESTIONS TO ASK YOURSELF

- How do others perceive me? How can I find out what they think?
- Who in the organisation could I model myself on?

QUESTION 15 # HOW DO I MANAGE MY CAREER AND PREPARE MYSELF FOR PROMOTION?

Why it's important: If you want to be successful, it's not enough to be good at your job – you also need to manage your career.

Many years ago a longitudinal survey was undertaken of Harvard graduates. After 25 years it was found that those who had sketched out a career plan while at university were more successful in financial terms than those who hadn't. Some people saw this as proof that planning led to better results. However, it can be argued that it was the strategic-thinking skills that the planners displayed that were the real reason for their success. Either way it seems obvious to me that if you know where you're going you stand a better chance of getting there – especially if you have a map to guide you.

But having an overarching strategic plan is not enough. You also need a series of principles that will guide your professional life on a daily basis. I've listed a few ideas below, but every manager should spend time identifying the principles by which they will manage their professional life.

WHAT TO DO

- Draw up a strategic plan for your career and identify targets of where you want to be in five yearly intervals (*see Question 29*) and list your lifetime ambitions.

- You are your own greatest asset (unless mommy or daddy left you a fortune). So invest in yourself. Obtain any trade or professional qualifications that your job requires. Then go one level higher. This may involve studying for an MA, MSc, MBA or a higher-level professional qualification. Your aim is to obtain a competitive advantage over those you are competing against in your organisation and wider industry.

- Try to become an expert in an area of work where there are few experts but a high demand (*see Question 3*). However, don't fall into the trap of becoming the boffin of the organisation. You will still need to demonstrate that you can go beyond your specialist knowledge and see problems and opportunities in organisational-wide terms (*see Question 2*).

- Learn all you can about yourself and how others see you (*see Question 6*). The more you understand yourself – what makes you tick, what annoys you, how you react in particular situations – the more control you can exercise over yourself. This is vital, as staff and other managers will quickly clock your weaknesses and use this knowledge to manipulate a reaction from you if you let them.

- To increase your productivity and find time to do those jobs that will get you noticed (*see Question 20*), make sure that you apply the advice given on time management (*see Question 4*).

- Learn to manage your boss (*see Question 8*) and become known to those managers above your boss. It will be they who decide if you are ready to step into your boss's position when s/he leaves.

- It's not so long ago since people were judged and pigeon-holed according to how they spoke. Accents may not be so important today but the ability to speak and write clearly are still essential. If you are weak in these areas, you need to do something about it. There are plenty of books and courses available that you can access.

- Presentations require a particular form of speaking and also writing (for slides and handouts). You must master the art of presentations if you want to impress staff and managers (*see Question 9*). If senior managers are present, use every presentation as an opportunity to lay down a marker for any future interviews that you may have with them.

- Get known throughout the organisation for what you and your team do (*see Question 25*). Build an image of someone who gets things done or does them differently to other managers. Even a simple thing like running meetings according to the advice contained in Questions 10 and 11 will be enough to get people talking about you.

- Develop a professional image (*see Question 14*) based on integrity. People follow those they trust. If through your actions you demonstrate that you treat people with respect, equality and fairness and that you will never exploit them or their ideas for your own benefit, you will quickly establish a reputation for integrity.

- Develop a network of contacts both within and outside the organisation. Use professional organisations, training, social events, and meetings with customers and suppliers to extend the range of people who are at least willing to 'take your calls'.

- Remain match-fit. Attend at least one interview a year, even if you are not thinking about moving jobs. Two a year would be better. Regular interviews will keep you informed about the market for your skills and what's on offer elsewhere, and help you identify any areas of knowledge or skills that you need to develop.

- Avoid burn-out. Work hard, but don't spend every waking hour either working or thinking about work. Take pleasure in your family/ friends. Keep fit by doing something you enjoy, not something that is mind-numbingly boring. Read regularly – it's the greatest way to escape the cares of work. Develop interests outside work. In other words, try to lead a balanced life.

QUESTIONS TO ASK YOURSELF

- How interesting am I to talk to? Do I only have one topic of conversation – work?
- What are the three things I want to achieve most from my career?

KEY MESSAGES TO TAKE FROM THIS SECTION

- Believe in yourself – because if you don't, why should anyone else?
- Your most valuable asset is yourself. Invest in your own professional, social and cultural development.
- Never con yourself as to the reality of the situation. While you may encourage others to believe that perception is reality, you must always remember that truth is reality.
- Properly applied time management is the only way to increase your productivity.
- Avoid symptom management. If you only tackle the symptoms, you will never eradicate the problem.
- Be open to new ideas and the possibility that you got it wrong.

SECTION 2

MANAGING PEOPLE

[To] inculcate in the common people the virtue of reverence, of doing their best and enthusiasm ... rule over them with dignity and they will be reverent; treat them with kindness and they will do their best; raise the good and instruct those who are backward and they will be imbued with enthusiasm.

Confucius, *Analects* 2.20

INTRODUCTION

A manager's primary task is to achieve results through the actions of others. Yet a surprising number of managers forget this and feel that they must do the majority of the work. Others don't trust their staff (*see Question 1*) and only delegate the grunt work to them. This is a recipe for poor performance, poor staff morale and a nervous breakdown (eventually) for the manager.

According to Peter Drucker, regarded by many as the only true genius that management studies has produced, a manager's role is to:

- organise staff
- set objectives
- motivate staff
- monitor results against targets and take corrective action when required
- develop people, including themselves.

Nowhere in that list does it say that the manager must do all or even most of the work. You add value by managing effectively, so learn to delegate (*see Question 12*).

The more you know about your staff, the more effective you will become as a manager. You will also find it easier to delegate the right tasks to the right people in the right way. So find out about their ambitions, interests and background.

Enhance your relationship with staff further by treating them with respect. You don't have to be religious to recognise the wisdom contained in the Golden Rule: 'Do unto others as you would have them do unto you'. Or to translate it into management terms: 'Treat others as you would like to be treated'.

If you show a genuine interest in your staff and treat them with respect, you are half way to becoming an effective manager.

HOW CAN I WIN THE RECRUITMENT LOTTERY AND CONSISTENTLY SELECT THE RIGHT PEOPLE?

Why it's important: The people in any organisation can be its greatest asset. But select the wrong people and they can become a costly liability.

Your success as a manager depends to a large degree on the quality of the people who work for you. Good staff can make an average manager look great and bad staff can make a great manager look very average.

Yet the selection of staff – despite using psychological testing, interviews, work-based simulations presentations, graphology and even astrology – remains a very hit and miss affair. It's still the case that at an interview the interviewer or panel often make a judgement about the person within the first two minutes. I think this tendency goes back to the days when our ancestors would come across a stranger in a jungle clearing and had 20 seconds to decide if they were a friend or someone who would kill them. To overcome this tendency, try the following.

WHAT TO DO

THE PRINCIPLES

- Promote from within whenever possible. Too many managers think that the staffing grass is greener outside their organisation. It isn't. Every organisation has its fair share of idiots and geniuses. Sometimes the same person embodies both!

- When possible, appoint someone who has already demonstrated that they can deliver results. Someone who:
  - has personal pride and won't want to let themselves down and by implication you;
  - is self-motivated, enthusiastic, and trustworthy;
  - can see the bigger picture;
  - possesses commonsense, because it's not that common and it's the foundation of good decision making.

- If you have to recruit from outside, select people who take pride in their work, are bright, engaging, enthusiastic and interesting, and have a proven record of achievement.

- If you are going to ask applicants to make a presentation or take part in a simulation, ensure that there is no inbuilt bias in favour of internal candidates.

THE DETAILS

- Know exactly what skills and characteristics you are looking for in an applicant and make sure the panel agree on these before the interviews start.
- Establish a rapport with the applicant.
- Don't talk too much. Let the applicant do the talking.
- Avoid leading and closed questions.
- Ask both general and specific questions and probe for further information.
- Look for evidence to support any claims that the person makes about themselves and their previous achievements.
- Clarify all answers that are unclear, for example asking 'Do you mean …?'
- Don't be afraid of silences. They are usually a sign that the applicant is finding it difficult to answer a question. How they handle that can be very revealing. Do they panic or can they think on their feet and supply a reasonable, if not perfect, answer?
- Encourage the applicant to ask questions. This will reveal just how much preparation they have put into the interview.
- Never select a person on the basis of potential; base selection on actual achievements. The world is full of people with unfulfilled potential. Take me, for example: I could have played for West Bromwich Albion (if only I'd had the talent).

QUESTIONS TO ASK YOURSELF

- How much reliance do I place on first impressions? Am I willing to let later evidence overturn my first impressions?
- Do I accept too easily what applicants say?

QUESTION 17 **HOW MUCH SHOULD I KNOW ABOUT THE DAY-TO-DAY WORK OF MY STAFF?**

Why it's important: Staff expect you to have some appreciation of what they do. Without it, you'll lose credibility and find staff reluctant to come to you with problems.

This is a question that often worries newly appointed managers. The myth that to be an effective manager you have to be able to do the job of everyone that reports to you is as hard to kill off as Dracula. It goes back to a time when people were expected to start at the bottom and work their way up to the top. Any rational person who took a moment to reflect on the complex nature of the modern working environment would immediately see that it's impossible for any person to be skilled in every job in a department, let alone the entire organisation.

However, that doesn't mean you can get by without some knowledge of what your staff do and an appreciation of the difficulties they face. Such knowledge is essential if you want to respond intelligently to their queries, understand the pressures they work under and enjoy a level of credibility with them. Rightly, staff think that if you don't understand what they do, how can you possibly understand them and the problems they face?

WHAT TO DO

- Depending on the number of staff you manage, either find the time to sit with each person individually or select a sample, and talk to them. Don't hold the meeting in your office. Go to where they work and let them tell you about what they do and the problems they face.

- Get a feel for the environment in which the person works. Is it a mad house with phones ringing and constant interruptions, or a haven of tranquillity?

- Spend about an hour or so with each person selected.

- Use MBWA (management by walking about) as a way to maintain contact and build relationships and knowledge (*see Question 48*).

- When a member of staff comes to you with a problem, ask them to outline it in as much detail as possible. Ask questions to clarify what they are saying if necessary.

- When they have finished, ask them what they think should be done. They may have more than one possible solution to the problem. Again, listen, ask questions and evaluate each solution.

- Summarise the problem and the possible solutions to it and confirm that your understanding of the situation is accurate.

- Based on what you already know about their work and what you have heard, select what appears to be the best solution. Use phrases like 'From what you've said it's clear that you have a good handle on the problem and I agree with you that x seems to be the best solution'. Recognition of the part that they played in the decision-making process will both motivate the person and enhance their self-confidence.

- If you lack trust or confidence in the person's abilities, you'll need to confirm both the nature of the problem and possible solutions with other members of staff before making a final decision.

QUESTIONS TO ASK YOURSELF

- Which essential functions/jobs do I need to understand first?
- Which members of staff are going to need the most support from me?

QUESTION 18 HOW CAN I INCREASE MY TEAM'S PRODUCTIVITY?

Why it's important: Managers are judged on the results (productivity) they and their team achieve.

Managers are judged by how productive they and their teams are. The pressure for greater productivity has increased in recent years and it's become common for managers to be asked to do more while seeing their staff and resources reduced. To achieve the highest level of productivity, both you and your team have to be switched on and committed. If you can achieve this then you will feed off each other's energy and a virtuous circle will be created.

WHAT TO DO
WORKING ON YOURSELF

- Lead by example:
  - Demonstrate commitment, enthusiasm and passion about your work. It's catching, just as lethargy, boredom and disinterest are.
  - Don't procrastinate – staff will pick up on procrastination and use it as an excuse for their own delayed actions. Exercise self-control: set targets for yourself and strive to meet them. Prioritise your work and tackle the most important tasks first.
  - Keep your working environment neat and tidy. That way you won't be tempted to clean up and organise things before you start work (my favourite displacement activity). You'll also be able to find things more quickly.
  - If you're working on something important or which requires a high level of concentration, get away from interruptions by decamping to another room.
  - Come to work ready to work. Don't arrive half dead because of lack of sleep – or worse – a hangover.
- Follow the advice given in Question 4 on how to manage your time and prioritise work, and share this knowledge with your staff.
- At the end of every day, week and month identify the important stuff that you need to work on the following day, week or month (*see Question 4*).
- Use effective delegation to improve your productivity (*see Question 12*).

WORKING WITH OTHERS

- Ensure that everyone knows what their responsibilities and targets are. Set deadlines and monitor performance (*see Question 29*), but don't over-manage. As a manager you should be more interested in results than in process. Therefore give staff a reasonable degree of autonomy in how they organise their work.

- Support your staff at all times, but also hold them to account when they fail to deliver.

- Encourage, motivate and reward staff, and recognise that just talking to them on a regular basis can be a significant motivator (*see Question 21*).

- Look at ways to improve team spirit as a prelude to increased productivity (*see Question 34*).

- Create an atmosphere in which people can enjoy and take pride in their work. Publicly recognise the achievements of staff and give praise when deserved.

- Supply your team with the best tools you can afford and train them in how to use them fully. At a minimum, ensure that everyone can use all facilities available to them, including computers and any other machinery they use (*see Question 19*).

- Spend less time in meetings. Make those that you hold more productive (*see Questions 10 and 11*).

QUESTIONS TO ASK YOURSELF

- Am I too comfortable in my job? Have I stopped challenging myself and my staff?

- What aspect of my team's work attracts the most criticism? What am I going to do about it?

QUESTION 19 HOW CAN I USE STAFF TRAINING AND DEVELOPMENT TO IMPROVE PERFORMANCE?

Why it's important: Every manager has a responsibility to develop their staff and themselves.

It is often said that an organisation's greatest asset is its staff. It's more accurate to say that potentially staff are an organisation's greatest asset. Too many organisations fail to train and develop their staff adequately. It's well known that in tough times the first two budgets to be cut are advertising and training.

You may believe that you already have a well-trained staff. But I'll bet that if they are using a computer system or complex machinery they are only using about 20 per cent of its capabilities to do their job. Why am I so sure? Because adults learn what they need to know and disregard what they think is superfluous. Once your staff became competent at their job, they stopped asking what else the system could do for them. Effectively they are wasting 80 per cent of the system's capabilities. Reduce that wastage and productivity will be increased.

WHAT TO DO

- It's common to find that managers are reluctant to go on training courses with their staff. Possibly this is because they don't want to be upstaged by a junior member of staff. If you want your staff to engage fully in training, you need to demonstrate your commitment to it and act as a role model. Besides, attending a training event with your staff is a great way to get to know them and to identify talent.

- Undertake a training needs analysis for each member of staff. Start by recording what level of skills the person currently has and compare this to the skills and knowledge that they require to perform their job to an excellent standard. The difference between the two is the skills and knowledge gap they need to close.

- In conjunction with the person, develop a training plan to close the gap. This may be no more than sitting with a more experienced member of staff or following an in-house training programme. But it may also mean going for more training from the company who supplied the system or machine they work with.

- Before the person attends any training course, agree a set of assessment outcomes that you expect them to achieve.

- Ensure that every task your team has to perform can be done by at least two people.

- If you followed the advice in Question 16 you will have employed ambitious and enthusiastic staff who are interested in a career. Don't stifle their ambition. Work with them to identify their aims and ambitions, and develop a plan for how they can reach their goals. This may involve gaining further trade or professional qualifications, or improving their supervisory, management, presentational, technical, strategic or analytical skills.

- You may not be able to support your staff financially or with time off to pursue their training, but you can be sympathetic to their request to leave 30 minutes early on their college night or for time off for revision and exams. If they do pass, congratulate them publicly.

QUESTIONS TO ASK YOURSELF

- When did I last attend a training and development session?
- Do I actively promote training for staff, or do I see their attendance on a course in terms of lost productivity?

QUESTION 20 # HOW CAN I STAMP OUT RECURRING PROBLEMS?

Why it's important: Recurring problems cost time and money. Eliminate them at source and you save on both.

There are one-off problems and there are recurring problems. One-off problems are by their nature unique and are usually caused by an individual mistake or a combination of rare events. As long as there are people, you're going to have one-off problems/mistakes. However, the quality guru Kaoru Ishikawa outlined a way to identify the cause/s of recurring problems, which is applicable to organisations in both the manufacturing and service sectors.

Ishikawa's approach involves drawing a skeleton of a fish. The head of the fish is used to record the problem. The backbone is the main process that is under review. From the backbone hang the fish's smaller bones. These are the sub-processes that contribute to the main process you are investigating. To identify the fault/s that is causing the problem, it's necessary to examine each of these sub-processes (smaller bones) as the cause/s could lie anywhere and/or be caused by a combination of problems in several sub-processes.

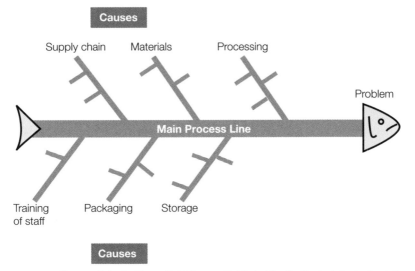

Source: Adapted from K. Ishikawa, *Guide to Quality Control*, 2nd edn, Asian Productivity Organization, 1968.

Obviously it's not necessary to draw a fish map – you could just as easily use a mind map or network chart to identify all the processes that you need to explore. Choose whichever approach you are most comfortable with.

WHAT TO DO

- Define your problem precisely and write it at the top of the page in or near the fish's head. For example, if customers are complaining about scratched products, is the problem caused by the actions of the carriers, is the packaging at fault, or are the materials used too susceptible to scratching?

- Analyse the causes of the problem using a small team to brainstorm the problem.

- Don't take action until you're sure you have identified the real problem and the sub-issues that make it up. You don't want to solve the problem you think exists – you want to eliminate the real thing.

- Remember, very often problems occur where two or more systems interface.

- Explore each 'bone' in turn, and exhaust your search of that bone before you move on to the next.

- As you identify each sub-problem, test and confirm that it actually contributes to the recurring problem.

- Log all problems that you identify, but put to one side those that don't contribute to the problem you are trying to fix. You can return to them later.

- Obtain the support of those you need to eliminate the problem (*see Question 45*). Don't antagonise people by blaming them for the problem. Instead, present the facts in neutral terms and show how a successful resolution can create a win/win situation for all parties (*see Question 23*).

- Identify a set of performance standards you can use to judge how effective your actions have been; for example, success = a reduction in customer complaints of 50 per cent (*see Question 29*).

- Don't claim all the credit for any improvement achieved – spread it around. That way colleagues and staff will be willing to help when you approach them for help next time.

QUESTIONS TO ASK YOURSELF

- What are the three worst recurring problems I currently face? What am I going to do about them?

- Who can help me identify all the potential causes of the problem?

QUESTION 21 HOW CAN I MOTIVATE STAFF?

Why it's important: Managers achieve results through their staff. A well-motivated staff deliver better and more consistent results than a demotivated team.

There are dozens if not hundreds of motivational theories to choose from. But before you can apply any of them there is one thing you need to do – you need to get to know your staff. Your staff are a collection of individuals and an approach that motivates one person may have no effect on another. That's why you need to know what makes each person tick. What are their likes, dislikes and interests? What do they value: is it money, status, or to be seen to have influence with you? The more you know about your team, the more effective your efforts at motivation will be.

Once you know your staff you can turn to motivation theories for further insights. Of all the theories around, I think that Frederick Herzberg's motivation and hygiene theory is the most practical to use. He identified genuine motivational factors and hygiene factors. Hygiene factors don't motivate staff, no matter how good they are, but they will demotivate staff if they fall below an acceptable level.

Factors that motivate staff	Hygiene factors that demotivate staff
Interesting, worthwhile work that challenges the individual	The working environment and staff facilities, when they fall below expected standards
Work that has meaning and value to the individual	Pay and job security, when they fall below peoples' expectations
A degree of responsibility and the autonomy to arrange and do the work in a way they choose	The organisation's rules, policies and procedures, when these obstruct work rather than assist performance
Recognition of good work and the possibility of advancement; this may involve promotion or being trusted with more complex work	Poor relations between staff and supervisors/managers

WHAT TO DO

- You can't motivate those who don't give a damn. So recruit committed, enthusiastic and self-motivated individuals who take a pride in themselves and their work (*see Question 16*).
- Use casual conversations, one-to-one meetings, team and performance review meetings, away days and social events to get to know your staff as people.
- Constantly monitor the hygiene factors and ensure that none of them falls below acceptable levels. What is acceptable will vary from organisation to organisation.
- Examine how work is distributed among staff. Is one person doing all the grunt tasks? If so, redistribute some of their work to others and give them a few interesting and challenging tasks to compensate for all the dross they still have to handle.
- Explain to staff how their work fits into the overall work flow and why it's important.
- Negotiate and set individual targets for each member of staff and allow staff a degree of autonomy in how they go about their work. Set a mixture of easy and challenging targets, as successful completion of the easier targets will motivate the person to tackle the harder targets.
- Whenever possible, promote from within (*see Question 16*). Do this constantly and people will see that advancement is possible if they work hard.
- Provide all staff with appropriate training and development opportunities (*see Question 19*).
- Remember to praise good work publicly. People may feel embarrassed, but that doesn't mean they don't want the recognition.

QUESTIONS TO ASK YOURSELF

- How well do I really know my staff?
- When was the last time that I thanked or praised a member of staff in private or in public?

HOW CAN I REWARD STAFF WHEN THE BUDGET IS TIGHT?

Why it's important: Staff should be recognised and rewarded for outstanding work. Failure to do so can demotivate and disillusion them.

The Hawthorne studies of motivation at General Electric in the 1920s and 1930s and the work of Herzberg in the 1960s (*see Question 21*) provide valuable insights into what people value and want from work. Surprisingly, both studies found that people valued non-financial rewards more highly than money. So while it's essential that people earn enough money to secure their basic needs, such as food, shelter and security, it is not the primary driving force that many believe it to be. There are numerous ways that you can reward staff, even when the budget is tight.

WHAT TO DO

- Staff want to be recognised for the good work they do. Public recognition of what they've achieved meets a deep need to feel valued and appreciated. So, remember that acknowledging good work in public, even if it's just saying 'Well done', can be enormously powerful.

- Talk to staff and include them in discussions about the way work is undertaken and the future direction of the team. This feeds into the individual's need to be recognised as a respected colleague rather than just a pair of hired hands.

- People are social animals and want to feel part of the pack. Encourage staff to feel that they are part of an elite team – the best in the organisation (*see Question 34*). They will quickly become proud of their status and they won't want to let their team mates down.

- Even if you can't actually promote someone, use the allocation of new, more interesting work or a greater level of autonomy as a way of recognising someone's work or achievements. For example, in my first job as a trainee accountant being given the number-two bank account to reconcile was a sign that I was now a fully fledged accounting assistant and not just the office junior. I received no pay rise but I can still remember the buzz it gave me ('What a sad soul', you must be thinking).

- Encourage people to invest in themselves by gaining trade and professional qualifications. Take a real interest in what they are doing and provide whatever support you can throughout their studies (*see Question 19*). Remember to publicise and celebrate their successes.
- Provide opportunities for in-house training and development (*see Question 19*). A great deal can be done with little or no money.
- Use the lack of money and the shared hardship that it brings as a means of uniting the team and building team spirit. Every military organisation in the world uses shared hardship during training as a means of building team spirit, and it's the basis of a lot of team-building exercises run by management development organisations.
- At your own expense, arrange some sort of gathering for your team. It doesn't have to cost a fortune. For example, you could have a summer barbeque or a pre-Christmas party at your place, a night at the dogs or a walk across a local beauty spot ending at a nice pub. I'm sure you can come up with better options.

QUESTIONS TO ASK YOURSELF

- Do I only think of rewards in terms of money and promotion?
- What non-financial rewards have I responded to positively in the past?

HOW CAN I HANDLE CONFLICT BETWEEN MEMBERS OF STAFF?

Why it's important: Like grit in the oyster, a little conflict can produce wonderful results. But too much is wholly destructive.

There are a number of ways that two parties may respond to a conflict.

RESPONSES TO CONFLICT:
Ignore the problem and pretend it doesn't exist. This results in tension and passive aggressive behaviour from both parties, leading to a lose/lose result.
Fight each other until one emerges victorious. This results in resentment on the part of the loser, and subsequent plots to get even, especially if their failure was public: a win/lose result.
Settle when one party decides to surrender and let the other have their way. This produces a lose/win result and ongoing discontent from one party.
Settle on a compromise solution, which involves both sides getting only some of what they wanted. This draw is not entirely satisfactory to either party and can lead to future skirmishes as people seek to set right imagined slights and injustices: a lose/lose outcome.
Reach consensus through a process of dialogue, mutual respect and a willingness to listen to others. A new solution is found that genuinely satisfies both parties, resulting in a win/win settlement.

Like competition, within a team a little conflict can be productive, as it can challenge entrenched views but if it should spill over into animosity then you have to take action.

WHAT TO DO

■ Encourage people to be open and frank. Let those who disagree with you or other team members have their say. But keep the discussion about work and step in if it becomes personal.

■ Don't ignore tension between colleagues. Find out the cause of the problem and monitor the situation. Only if the people involved show no sign of resolving their differences should you step in.

■ If you decide to intervene, talk to staff not involved in the situation first. Their views will be biased but at least they are not as emotionally involved in the dispute as the main combatants.

■ Start by speaking to the individuals involved separately. If you go for a joint meeting you run the risk of releasing all the pent-up anger of the parties involved. Better they work through some of that anger with you before a joint meeting. Treat this meeting as a scoping exercise and identify what the real issues are behind all the emotion and anger on display.

■ Call a meeting of the parties involved and if required have someone sit in to take notes.

■ Start by outlining the problem as you see it. Then give each person the opportunity to outline their case without interruption.

■ Your aim is to reach a consensus – a win/win result. If you can't achieve this, aim for a compromise solution that will hold in the medium term while you continue to pursue a win/win outcome.

■ To achieve consensus, you'll have to come up with a solution that gives both parties what they want. Very often work disputes are about the methods used to achieve an objective, not the objective itself. Therefore start by defining the final outcome that both parties are agreed on and work backwards from there to achieve consensus.

QUESTIONS TO ASK YOURSELF

■ How comfortable am I dealing with conflict? Do I need training in conflict resolution?

■ What's my usual response to a member of staff disagreeing with me?

HOW CAN I GIVE NEGATIVE FEEDBACK TO STAFF WITHOUT DEMOTIVATING THEM?

Why it's important: To improve someone's performance, you have to tell them where they are currently going wrong and how they can put it right.

The advice here about giving negative feedback is equally applicable to cases of poor timekeeping or attendance as it is to poor work performance or arriving hung over at work.

It's important to realise that many people have delusions of adequacy or importance. They are convinced that they do a wonderful job and that without them the organisation would collapse. Others have no interest in their work and do the bare minimum to get by. You can't afford to carry any of these passengers. At some stage you may have to involve the human resources department in formal disciplinary action. But before you do that, a metaphorical kick up the pants from you, in the form of some frank feedback, may resolve the problem.

Feedback has got a new trendy name – it's now called feed-forward. I think it's a terrible term, but it does highlight the most important purpose of feedback. Feedback is meant to improve a person's future performance. It's not about holding the person to account for every mistake they've ever made. A successful session should leave the participant motivated to do better.

If used correctly, feedback can be one of the most effective ways to develop staff. And the good news is that by following just a few guidelines it can be a relatively easy and stress-free process – for you at least.

WHAT TO DO

- Read this question in conjunction with Question 26.

- Provide feedback as soon as possible after the event to which it relates. If you catch someone doing something good, say 'Well done'. You'll be amazed at the effect it has on them. If you see someone making a minor error, have a quiet word with them.

- Where the problem is more significant, arrange a feedback meeting quickly. Don't wait. Hold the meeting when the events or issues are fresh in everyone's mind.

- However, never hold the meeting when you are angry or upset. In this case a small delay can allow any anger or emotion associated with the problem to recede. It also gives you time to identify how you want the person to behave in future.

- Hold the meeting in private, on neutral ground and if possible without interruptions.

- During the meeting, don't criticise the person. Comment only on their actions. The divide between the person and their actions can be difficult to maintain but it's essential if rampant emotion is to be kept at bay.

- Try using the 'crap sandwich' approach to structure your feedback: start with something positive, move on to the critical, and then finish with another slice of positivity.

- Outline the actions/behaviours that have caused you concern. Ask the person if they wish to comment on what you've said, but don't enter into a discussion or argument – just listen.

- If appropriate, take on board what the person has said, for example if they want to correct some factual error. But don't take on board self-serving emotional appeals or excuses.

- Outline clearly what steps the person must take to improve their work. Record this in an action plan and give them a copy. Finish by explaining what will happen if improvement isn't achieved.

- If required, arrange a future meeting to discuss progress against plan.

QUESTIONS TO ASK YOURSELF

- How often do I give feedback to my staff on their performance?

- When was the last time I publicly acknowledged the good work of a member of staff?

QUESTION 25 # HOW CAN I GET MY TEAM AND MYSELF NOTICED BY THE PEOPLE THAT MATTER?

Why it's important: Doing your job well is not sufficient if you want to get promoted. You have to stand out from the crowd.

Managers are not judged solely on what they do but also on what their team achieves. The proof of your management skills is reflected in how good your team is. If your team is performing badly, it means you are not doing your job. Your job is to knock your team into shape, using any and all means available to you. But the door of responsibility swings both ways. If your team has a great reputation, it's only right that you get credit for that. So you are not being entirely altruistic when you seek recognition for your team. There is also an element of self-promotion.

WHAT TO DO

- Identify who the real power brokers are in the organisation who can affect your career. Then identify when, where and how you come in contact with them and target these occasions as opportunities for getting noticed (*see Question 45*).

- Singing your own praises isn't very attractive. Nor is it always effective. It can annoy the people you want to impress. Therefore use the term 'my team' more often than 'I'.

- If you are asked to write a report, which will be circulated to those you want to impress, address the issues discussed in terms of how they affect both your department and the wider organisation. This will demonstrate that you have what Charles Handy calls the helicopter factor. This mindset allows you to rise above parochial problems/ opportunities and consider the issue in organisational terms. This ability – more than any other – marks managers out as prospective executives/directors (*see Question 2*).

- If you give a presentation attended by power brokers (*see Question 9*) use it as an opportunity to showcase the work of your team as well as your own communication and presentational skills. As with your written report, demonstrate that you have the helicopter factor. If you are aware of a particular broker's pet interests, include something in your presentation that will attract their interest.

- If possible lead a high-profile cross-department project team (*see Section 3*). The upside of this is that, if you're successful, you'll be noticed and your reputation will grow. But remember that if you fail you might find yourself side-lined or find yourself out of a job.

- Interdepartmental projects are a great opportunity to show that you can operate outside your professional discipline as a general manager. Unfortunately, many excellent managers fail to make the transition to general management because after promotion they continue to view problems through the lens of their own specialist area. This leads to sub-optimisation when decisions requiring cross-organisational thinking are made. If you can demonstrate that you are not a prisoner to your professional background, you position yourself as someone to watch.

- In any meetings with power brokers, always demonstrate confidence in yourself and your team, especially if you're nervous. How you feel is unimportant – it's how you are perceived that counts. You must look as if you belong in such company.

QUESTIONS TO ASK YOURSELF

- What am I and my team currently doing above and beyond our remit, which I need to advertise?
- Do I consistently promote the achievements of my team?

QUESTION 26   # HOW CAN I TURN AROUND AN UNDERPERFORMING GROUP OF STAFF?

Why it's important: Whether it's a project team or the group of people you manage every day, it's essential that your staff act as a team if you and they are to be successful.

Douglas McGregor, author of *The Human Side of Enterprise*, identified the features of ineffective teams. Nearly every problem you encounter with your team will fall into one of the following categories.

FAILING TEAMS:

Are dominated by their manager and have little autonomy in how they manage their work.

Are disinterested and bored by the work they are doing.

Lack a clear set of targets and objectives.

Are dominated by the views of one or two key people in the group.

Show little respect for team members or what they say.

Use majority voting when making decisions, rather than seek genuine consensus.

Discourage the sharing of feelings in public and see criticism or conflict with other team members as something to avoid.

Avoid discussion about their actions or how effective they are.

WHAT TO DO

- Don't micro-manage your team. Your staff are adults and expect some discretion in how they manage their work (*see Question 21*). Agree with each person the limits of their discretion and then get out of their way and let them surprise you. As the person develops, extend the limits of their discretion. If they constantly mess up tasks, reduce the limits.

- People are motivated by interesting work that they believe is meaningful (*see Question 21*). Show each member of the team how their work contributes to the overall production of the team and how failure to complete the work to a high standard reduces overall efficiency.

- There are always boring tasks that have to be undertaken in any team. Don't give all the rubbish jobs to one person. Share them around. Even do a few yourself.

- Ensure that your team, and every person in it, has a clear set of targets and objectives that are fully aligned with the organisation's goals. Then implement an effective monitoring system that ensures that any slippage is identified and dealt with early (*see Question 29*).

- Run your team meetings using the principles outlined in Questions 10 and 11. But don't dominate proceedings. Let the staff do most of the talking. Emphasise the need for everyone to contribute, and make it clear that the views of everyone should be respected.

- Lead by example. Demonstrate that you would rather reach consensus on an idea than make a decision based on a show of hands or without consulting staff. (Though there will be some occasions when you have to make the decision on your own.)

- Encourage staff in team meetings to evaluate critically the work of the group. This should include an examination of how effectively the team works, what it has done and what it has failed to do in the past x weeks, and how it could do better in the future. Allow staff to criticise both themselves and others in the group, but ensure that the criticism never becomes personal (*see Question 23*).

QUESTIONS TO ASK YOURSELF

- What systems do I have in place to measure how effective my team is (*see Question 29*)?

- Which of my actions contribute to the team's poor performance?

WHAT SHOULD I BE DOING AT EACH STAGE OF THE CHANGE PROCESS?

Why it's important: You need to know the key stages of the change cycle and what people are feeling at each stage if you are to manage the process successfully.

There are almost as many change management cycles as there are writers on the subject. Based upon observation and the delivery of numerous projects my own model contains seven stages:

CHANGE CYCLE:

Disbelief: The person is convinced that there has been a mistake and that nothing will change.

Bewilderment, fear and aggression: The person finally accepts that change is coming but can't understand why it's required or their role in the future.

Resistance: The person digs their heels in and tries to stop, delay or change what is proposed so as to minimise the effect it will have on them.

Searching: As the threat becomes firmed up, the person identifies what their new role will be and consciously tries to fit it into a version of their old job.

Surrender: The person comes to terms with their new role and stops fighting. They surrender to the inevitable but still hanker after the past.

Internalisation: The change has been implemented and the person has internalised their changed duties and their redefined role in the organisation.

Moving on: The new role has become the norm and the person acts accordingly – until the next change.

Unfortunately people don't move through the process in a straight line. They may get stuck at a particular stage or even regress to an earlier stage. Such regressions may be required in order to deal with unresolved issues before people can progress to acceptance and internalisation of the change.

WHAT TO DO

- As soon as the change is proposed, establish an implementation team that includes staff who are trusted by their colleagues and who can act as change champions.

- Brief the change champions and explain that their job is to promote the change, answer questions, dispel rumours and provide feedback to you.

- Recognise that a willingness to communicate with staff until you've lost your voice is a prerequisite to successful change. Make yourself available to every member of staff and use every opportunity you get to explain, reassure and placate staff.

- Use MBWA (management by walking about) to communicate with staff and listen to their concerns (see Question 48). Emphasise that the change will take place and alleviate any fears by providing opportunities for staff to discuss their fears with colleagues, supervisors and yourself.

- Use your knowledge of the staff to encourage, guide and help staff through the change (see Question 21). Remember that people will progress through the cycle at different speeds.

- To reassure staff that they have a future, start retraining people as soon as possible.

- Give people a forum in which they can vent their anger and frustration. This forum can be public or private.

- Don't compromise on what has to be done, but be open to any suggestions that will minimise the unintended effects of the change. Acceptance of even a minor suggestion can help individuals enormously.

- Constantly reassure staff that their future is going to be better than the past and that you believe that they have an important part to play in the organisation's progress.

- Mark the end of the change by celebrating and acknowledging all the hard work that staff and the change team have put in.

QUESTIONS TO ASK YOURSELF

- How do I feel about change? Do I like or fear change?
- Do my staff feel the same way?

QUESTION 28 HOW DO I DEAL WITH THOSE PEOPLE WHO OPPOSE CHANGE?

Why it's important: Like the proverbial bad apple, one person committed to resisting change can sour the contents of an entire barrel.

Let's be clear here we're not talking about people who find change difficult. We are talking about that small number of staff who actively oppose the change and wish to block it. By all means try to persuade them of the benefits of the change, but if they remain firm in their opposition consider using what the Pulitzer-Prize-winner James MacGregor Burns termed transactional management. Transactional management involves either offering the person an inducement to comply with your wishes (a constructive transaction) or threatening them with a sanction (a coercive transaction). Essentially it's a form of bartering and as such has existed since a caveman swapped an axe and two spears for the new-fangled weapon called the bow.

Constructive transactions occur when:	Corrective or coercive transactions occur when:
The manager offers inducements to the member of staff in return for compliance, e.g. 'If you work with me on this change I'll see what I can do about promoting you/giving you the window desk/your own office'.	The manager threatens the member of staff with a sanction if they continue to oppose the change, e.g. 'This change is going to happen and if you don't engage with the process you may find that your future promotion prospects are damaged'.

WHAT TO DO

- Before you mention either constructive or coercive transactions, identify the limits of your power (*see Question 3*). It's essential that whatever action you take you can deliver on your promise/threat – otherwise you'll lose credibility.

- Before you take any action, meet with the person and explore their reasons for opposition to the change. Their opposition may be based on a misunderstanding, in which case you can resolve it. But more likely there is a deeper personal or psychological issue in play. If you can identify this, you are half way to resolving the problem. But to do so you'll have to win the person's trust (*see Question 14*) and be willing to listen not only to what they say but the sub-text of what they say.

- If discussion doesn't work, find out what motivates the person (*see Question 21*). What do they value? What do they fear? The more you can tailor your offer/threat, the greater impact it will have on the person.

- Always start with a constructive transaction. Offer the person something you know they want/value in return for their co-operation.

- If you can't reach an agreement or a compromise, lay out the coercive actions that could follow, should the person continue to oppose the change. Be very careful that nothing you say can be interpreted as either bullying or the basis for a constructive dismissal claim.

- Should they persist in opposing the change, you may need to involve human resources and discipline the person for failing to carry out a reasonable request by management. Try to avoid this if possible, as it casts them in the light of martyr and they can become a rallying point for other discontented staff.

QUESTIONS TO ASK YOURSELF

- How successful/unsuccessful have I been in gaining staff compliance in the past? Which strategies were most/least successful?

- How flexible am I when it comes to making minor adjustments to my plans?

QUESTION 29 HOW DO I SET TARGETS FOR MYSELF AND MY STAFF?

Why it's important: Managers are judged on what they deliver, not on how popular they are.

You can be the most affable colleague in the world, but unless you can deliver results you'll never make it. To deliver great results you need the active support of your staff. As part of your motivation strategy (*see Question 21*) you should set both team and individual targets for your staff.

Unfortunately, many managers spend insufficient time thinking about how they should frame their targets. The result is that they end up with a wish list that lacks clarity, is overly ambitious, often self-contradictory, unachievable and lacking in completion dates. You need to avoid such pitfalls.

You will be familiar with the idea of SMART targets. John Whitmore expanded upon these to develop a more comprehensive target-setting model:

TARGET SETTING:

SMART targets are: Specific, Measurable, Achievable, Realistic and Timed.

PURE targets are: Positively stated, Understandable, Relevant and Ethical.

CLEAR targets are: Challenging, Legal, Environmentally sound, Agreed with staff and Recorded.

The SMART list contains the criteria your targets must meet if they are to be effective in practice. The PURE list provides guidance on how targets should be written. The CLEAR list interrogates your targets and asks that you confirm they pass five tests: i.e. are they challenging, are they legal, etc.

WHAT TO DO

■ Start by keeping a record of recurring problems, complaints received and any concerns you have about poor economy, efficiency or effectiveness (*see Questions 20 and 65*). Use these notes to draw up your own targets.

- Combine your list of targets with those delegated to you by your boss. Involve your staff as early as possible in the discussions about targets. Working with your team, break down each target into a series of interim targets or milestones.

- Specify a completion date for each milestone. Achievement of a milestone will both motivate you and your staff and act as a check on progress.

- Your top priorities are the targets set by your boss. These are the ones you must achieve.

- Below them prioritise your own targets according to which will benefit the organisation the most. Be realistic about what you can achieve in the time available. Better to achieve two of your own targets than partially achieve four.

- Use the criteria outlined in Whitmore's target-setting model to help you write a set of clear, robust and realistic targets.

- Hold regular monthly monitoring meetings and devise a simple reporting system that will enable you to monitor progress, identify problems and record any corrective action that is agreed upon. For example, a monthly target/actual report could look like this:

Annual target	Interim target to 30/4/XX	Actual to 30/4/XX	Variance pos./neg.	Action required by next meeting on 30/5/XX
Reduce complaints to 9,000 per year	3,000	2,500	500 pos.	Patrick to identify reasons for good performance and determine to what extent this can be built upon

QUESTIONS TO ASK YOURSELF

- Have I got the required support of staff and stakeholders to achieve each target?

- Have I got the resources required to achieve each target?

QUESTION 30   # HOW DO MY STAFF PERCEIVE THEIR RELATIONSHIP WITH MANAGEMENT?

Why it's important: How people think they are perceived by management affects their performance.

Question 21 looked at which factors motivate/demotivate staff. How effective the motivational factors are will depend on how the member of staff feels about the organisation they work for. If they feel that they are not trusted or respected by the organisation/management, it is very unlikely that you will be able to motivate them.

Research within a university faculty in 2002/3 found that how people perceived their relationship with the management of the faculty affected significantly their level of motivation. When people felt that they were respected and trusted by management, they were happy and well motivated in their work. However, when they perceived that the organisation did not trust or respect them they lacked motivation and felt aggrieved.

Four possible perceptions of the relationship between staff and management were identified:

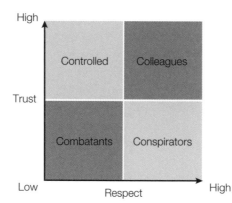

Source: J. McGrath, 'Leading in a Managerialist Paradigm: A Survey of Perceptions within a Faculty of Education', doctoral thesis, University of Birmingham, 2004.

- **Controlled**: Staff who are trusted because they don't rock the boat and do as they are told, but they are not particularly respected by managers because they have few ideas of their own.
- **Colleagues**: Staff who are both trusted and respected by management because their views and beliefs about how the organisation should be run coincide with those of management.
- **Conspirators**: Staff who are not trusted because they hold different views to management about how the organisation should be run, but are respected because they either possess expert knowledge (*see Question 3*) and/or they are highly competent workers.
- **Combatants**: Staff who are at war with the organisation, sometimes for personal reasons. They are seen as troublemakers and are neither trusted nor respected by management.

WHAT TO DO

- Remember that staff see their immediate manager as representative of the organisation's management. Therefore, they will project on to you their feelings about the organisation and how it treats them.
- Remember also that the above describes how staff think management sees them. In reality management may hold a very different view of the person. However, the person doesn't know this and acts as if their perception is both real and correct.
- Through observing what staff do and how they interact with colleagues, other managers and yourself, try to identify which group the person thinks they belong to. Then hold a meeting with them to discuss how they feel about their work, the organisation and where they see themselves going over the next five years. Keep this meeting light and informal. Use the meeting to get to know the person (*see Question 21*) and as a way to confirm (as far as you can) your assessment of how the person perceives their relationship with the organisation.
- Once you have a fair idea of how staff perceive their relationship with the organisation, you need to support those who see themselves as colleagues, while still being willing to criticise their actions when necessary (*see Question 24*).
- For those who see themselves as conspirators, combatants or controlled, you need to start work repairing their relationship with the

organisation. This begins with you establishing a relationship based on mutual trust and respect.

- How you handle the establishment of this new relationship will depend on whether you are a new manager or one who has been in post for some time. A new manager can announce that all staff start with a clean slate as far as they are concerned.

- To get the same message across to a group of staff you have been managing for a few years will require a more subtle approach. Remember that actions speak louder than words. Use any interactions you have with staff to demonstrate your trust and respect. Give praise where it is due and be willing to listen to both the problems that staff bring to you and any ideas that they have for how the team's economy, efficiency and effectiveness can be improved (*see Questions 18 and 65*).

- Always give the staff credit for what they have done and don't steal their ideas and call them your own.

QUESTIONS TO ASK YOURSELF

- Using the twin measures of trust and respect, how do I see each member of my team? What evidence do I have for making such judgements?
- Do my judgements affect how I treat staff?

KEY MESSAGES TO TAKE FROM THIS SECTION

- Staff are potentially your greatest asset – treat them as such.
- Develop a reasonable knowledge of industrial relations and employment law. It will help you avoid expensive legal actions.
- Get to know your staff – their strengths, weakness, likes and dislikes. Treat people as individuals. Take the trouble to remember their birthdays and the names of their partner and children, etc.
- Maintain a professional distance from your staff. You can be friendly and approachable, but at some stage you may have to take disciplinary action against a member of staff or sack them.
- Remember that the best ideas can come from the most junior member of staff. Provide opportunities for them to raise their ideas.
- You have a responsibility to support and develop your staff.

SECTION 3

MANAGING PROJECTS

If [I] were leading the Three Armies … I would not take with me anyone who would fight a tiger with his bare hands … and die in the process without regret. If I took anyone it would be a man who, when faced with a task, was fearful of failure and who, while fond of making plans, was capable of successful execution.

Confucius, *Analects* 7.11

INTRODUCTION

Too many managers who are appointed to executive-level posts continue to view the problems they face through the lens of their own profession. So we have the situation where the accountant looks at a problem from a financial position, an engineer frames the issue in engineering terms and the marketing director sees it as a marketing issue. What they all need to do is see the problem in organisation-wide terms and tackle the problem in its entirety and not just look at selected facets of it.

This section is about managing project teams. Often such teams are cross-disciplinary and/or cross-departmental. They are a great opportunity for you to exercise your management muscles as a general manager and to show senior executives that you have what it takes to step up to executive level.

Unfortunately, projects are risky and if you fail it can tarnish your reputation and set you back. But this should not dissuade you from grabbing such opportunities by the throat and throttling them into submission. Remember, failure is very often the price you pay for future success. We learn from our successes but we learn more from setbacks – provided we take responsibility for them and identify why things went wrong and what we need to do differently in the future.

When managing a project you want people in your team who you can depend on. People who take pride in their work and are ready to do whatever's required to avoid failure. They plan their actions and don't rush off half-cocked. But they also understand that too much planning can cause delay and recognise that they must take action to get the job done. They are not heroes ready to embrace glorious failure – they are pragmatists who finish the job. So avoid bare-handed tiger fighters.

WHAT ARE THE THREE RULES OF PROJECT MANAGEMENT?

Why it's important: You need to get the basics right if your project is to have any chance of success.

Kelly Johnson famously devised 14 rules and practices for project work at the aircraft manufacturer Lockheed Martin. Many of these rules related to the working practices of the company, but contained within his advice were three rules that are essential to the good management of all projects.

JOHNSON'S THREE RULES OF PROJECT MANAGEMENT:

The number of people employed on the project must be kept to the minimum. The more people there are, the more complex communication and control become.

Meetings must be kept to a minimum. Ideally there should be a weekly team meeting to review progress and consider if any changes to the project are required and a monthly meeting between the project manager and project sponsors. Further meetings are counterproductive and increase admin.

Only two regular reports should be produced. Weekly, the project team should receive a progress report detailing progress to date against plan. Monthly, the sponsors should receive a copy of the most up-to-date progress report and a detailed project finance report. Any additional reports take up time that can be better spent working on the project.

WHAT TO DO

- Keep your team small and manageable. This will aid communication and clarity of purpose within the team. In addition, team spirit and group identity is established more quickly within small teams.

- Once the project is up and running and it looks like it's going to be a success, you'll be amazed how many glory hunters will want to jump on the band wagon. Repel all boarders.

- Hold a single, short progress meeting with the project team each Friday afternoon or Monday morning. Use the meeting to monitor progress against plan and to prioritise the next week's work.

- Learn to say *no*.

- At the weekly progress meeting, reject all requests for changes or enhancements to the project unless they are absolutely essential. Record all suggestions made as issues to be dealt with in any Phase 2 of the project.

- At the end of the month, table a budget/actual report at the team meeting and take corrective action as required (*see Question 60*).

- At the end of each team meeting, list the 'must achieve targets' for the following week.

- At the monthly sponsors' meeting, present the latest progress report and a project budget report. The budget report should compare the spending to date against budget and provide details of committed, but not yet incurred, expenditure and a forecast of total costs to the end of the project.

- Other than providing your sponsors with the information they require, your main task at these meetings will be to say no to suggestions for how the project could be improved. Stick to your guns. Take on board and record all suggestions but make it clear that unless the suggestion can be shown to make achievement of the original aim easier/quicker it will have to wait until Phase 2 (*see Question 41*).

- Build alliances with key sponsors who will support you when you say no (*see Question 41*).

- Remember, if you say yes to changes and the project is delayed, it will be you who carries the can, not the person who made the suggestion.

QUESTIONS TO ASK YOURSELF

- How assertive am I when dealing with senior management?
- Who among the senior management can help me say no to proposed project changes?

QUESTION 32 WHAT AM I SUPPOSED TO DO AS PROJECT LEADER?

Why it's important: Project managers are usually told what they have to achieve, but they are seldom given any guidance on their role and responsibilities. It's assumed they know what is required.

If you read many of the job descriptions for a project manager, the role seems to be beyond the capacity of any mere mortal. The truth is that, as with any management role, the job is about working with people. Establish good relationships with the sponsors of the project and your project team, and you are more than half way home.

THE EIGHT MAJOR FUNCTIONS OF EVERY PROJECT MANAGER:

Complete the project successfully, on time and within budget.

Define and agree the scope of the project with senior management.

Select and build an effective project team (senior management may have their views on who to include).

Produce a detailed plan for the project with the aid of the team members.

Ensure that the project is adequately resourced.

Manage the project on a day-to-day basis.

Motivate the team members.

Monitor the project to ensure that it remains on target, within budget and executed to the required standard.

WHAT TO DO

- Your single most important function as project manager is to complete the project successfully, on time and within budget. How you do it is up to you, but do it you must.

- Start by defining the scope of the project with senior management and agreeing a set of criteria against which the success of the project will be assessed (*see Question 29*). Record what has been agreed in writing and use this to combat requests for changes to the project (*see Question 41*).

- Have in your head a clear picture of what the final project will look like. You need to be able to describe it to others in just a few sentences – your vision for the project (*see Question 59*).

- Good managers surround themselves with good people. So fill the roles required with reliable people who have a record of success, hate failure and have the skills required (*see Question 16*).

- Save the detailed project planning until you've established your team. The team members can help you devise a plan that is based upon reality and not wishful thinking or guesswork. In addition, working through the issues will help the team to gel and ensure that the team owns the plan (*see Question 34*).

- As project manager there will be times when you have to get stuck in and help the staff. But your main priorities are to provide the resources that the team needs to do its job and keep extraneous events and demands from disrupting its work.

- To maintain progress you need to maintain staff morale and motivation (*see Question 21*). This includes knowing when you need to say 'OK guys. That's enough. Let's go down the pub.'

- Hold a weekly team meeting to monitor progress and prioritise work for the week ahead (*see Question 31*).

- Hold a monthly meeting with the project sponsors. Report progress to date against plan and spending to date against budget (*see Question 39*).

QUESTIONS TO ASK YOURSELF

- Do I have a clear mental image of what a successful project will look like?

- Do the members of my team share the same image?

QUESTION 33 — WHAT MIX OF SKILLS AND ATTITUDES DOES MY PROJECT TEAM NEED?

Why it's important: If your team does not possess the necessary mix of skills and attitudes, you will find it difficult/impossible to complete the project.

Meredith Belbin suggests that there are nine roles that must be filled in any team.

BELBIN'S TEAM ROLES:

The chair who manages the team – you.

Shapers need to be strategic thinkers who are comfortable making decisions and don't mind ruffling a few feathers if that gets the job done.

Plants are original thinkers. They like to innovate, solve problems and generate ideas.

Monitors are analytical. They are objective and seldom let feelings affect their decisions. They can appear cold and unemotional and be critical of team mates.

Implementers are the team's workhorses. They want to get on with the job but they can find it hard to compromise, which can cause tensions.

Resource investigators are the scroungers of the team. If you need resources they'll find them – just don't ask them how they did it.

Team workers are social animals and want everyone to be happy. They are great at resolving conflict within the team.

Completers are driven by achievement of their objectives and don't take prisoners if someone blocks them. They'll do what is required to complete the project.

Specialists provide the expert knowledge and skills that are required to complete the project. They can sometimes appear aloof to other members.

In small teams one person may cover more than one role.

As well as appointing people with the right skills ensure that they have the right attitude. See Question 16 for a description of the type of people you want in your team.

WHAT TO DO

- As the chair you need to ensure that you manage and motivate the team. Set the agenda for the team and remain calm, confident and supportive, even when things go wrong.
- You may not be able to choose your own team. The project sponsors may do it for you. In which case evaluate 'your team' against the criteria above and negotiate the removal of as many square pegs as you can. The sponsors are unlikely to argue with you if you can demonstrate that their choice/s could undermine the project.
- If you are free to select your own team then choose people who you trust and know can deliver. If you have to choose from strangers, hold informal interviews and use the descriptors shown above and in Question 16 to guide your choices.
- Remember that if the project team is small, one person may have to fill two or more roles.
- If you are managing a large-scale project, allow the section leaders to select their own staff. They will know what they are looking for, and it will demonstrate your trust in the team.
- Remember what Kelly Johnson said about keeping the number of people to a minimum. Don't include anyone in the team who doesn't have a clearly defined purpose (*see Question 31*).

QUESTIONS TO ASK YOURSELF

- Who has the final say over membership of the project team?
- Have I got the power to 'sack' someone from the team?

QUESTION 34 HOW DO I BUILD TEAM SPIRIT?

Why it's important: Great team spirit helps people to go beyond their self-imposed limits.

There are a number of concepts that are very difficult to define – for example, beauty, leadership and justice – but you recognise them immediately when you see them. The same is true of team spirit. Without team spirit, a group of six people will produce the work of six people. With team spirit, synergy occurs and suddenly the team is producing the work of eight or more people.

The advice given below is equally applicable to a project team or the team of people you work with every day.

WHAT TO DO

- Get to know your team as individuals. The more you know about each person the better.
- Discover what motivates and demotivates each person (*see Question 21*) and use this knowledge to shape your interactions with individuals and the entire team.
- Set realistic targets as part of the project-planning process. Monitor progress and hold those who fail to account. Celebrate when people meet or exceed their target (*see Question 29*).
- Praise people for good work – and whenever possible do it in public. Encourage team members to offer both praise and criticism to colleagues during your weekly project management meeting (*see Question 21*). As shown by the Hawthorne experiments, this makes people feel valued and increases their sense of belonging to the group.
- Provide both positive and negative criticism as required (*see Question 24*). Don't do as some trainers suggest and only provide positive feedback. If everyone and everything is wonderful then praise becomes meaningless.
- Encourage open communication. Make yourself available to staff: get out of your office as much as possible and be seen. Don't call people into your office – go to them. Keep your door open and be ready to talk to staff.
- Listen to any ideas that staff have and implement their suggestions

in whole or part. It will give them and the rest of the team a boost to know that they can make a difference.

- Model the type of behaviour that you want your team to display and treat everyone with courtesy, dignity and respect. Get rid of troublemakers or those that don't fit in.
- Show that you trust the team and delegate work that people will find interesting and rewarding (see Question 12).
- Provide the resources your team needs to do the job. Nothing is more frustrating for people than to find that they are delayed because of missing equipment.
- Within any good team there is bound to be an element of conflict, with committed people holding opposing views as to how to do things. Encourage a healthy level of productive conflict, but know when to step in (see Question 23).
- Have a laugh. Work is serious but that doesn't mean that the people performing it have to be. If you can't enjoy work, what's the point?
- Celebrate even small successes.
- Arrange for the team to meet socially outside work, and either charge the occasion to the organisation or foot the bill yourself (see Question 22).

QUESTIONS TO ASK YOURSELF

- Do I pay enough attention to building team spirit or am I focusing too much on tasks and targets?
- What activity outside work could I use to build team spirit?

QUESTION 35 # HOW DO I PLAN A PROJECT AND SET MILESTONES?

Why it's important: A plan provides you with a road map and enables you to monitor progress.

There is a balance to be struck between too little and too much planning. All plans are forward looking and no one can predict the future. Therefore all plans are inherently inaccurate. So don't try to produce the perfect plan. Aim to produce the equivalent of a good hand-drawn map. This will allow you to make the occasional detour without losing sight of your ultimate aim.

Two tools can help your analysis and planning. First, when you are appointed project manager, use Geoff Round's TRAP model to do a quick and dirty analysis of the project.

ANALYSING A PROJECT:

Task: Confirm and clarify the task.

Resources: Confirm and clarify what resources (human and material) you have.

Arithmetic: Check that the arithmetic adds up; i.e. given the task and the timescale for its completion, are the resources provided sufficient to do the job?

Priorities: Identify what the project's priorities are.

At the first meeting of your project team, you can then start the detailed planning.

PLANNING A PROJECT:

Stage 1: Identify in as much detail as possible the purpose of the project. You and your team must be able to describe the project's ultimate aim in a sentence.

Stage 2: Split your aim into a series of interim objectives. These will be significant pieces of work (milestones), which, if achieved, move you closer to the achievement of your aim.

Stage 3: Take each objective in turn and decide what tasks and targets you need to complete or meet to achieve your objective.

Stage 4: Decide who will be responsible for the completion of each task. Use Whitmore's target-setting model (*see Question 29*) to identify the criteria that have to be met for a task, target or milestone to be achieved.

Stage 5: Set up a monitoring system that allows progress to be compared with what was planned (*see Question 29*).

Stage 6: On completion of the project, record any lessons learnt that might help future project teams, and take time to celebrate the team's work.

WHAT TO DO

- Based on your TRAP analysis, decide if the project is a goer or a poisoned chalice. Renegotiate with your sponsors if required.
- Work through each of the six stages outlined above and use the expertise in the room to fully explore the issues that arise. This process will help the team to gel and to buy into the plan as something they helped to create.
- At different stages of planning you may need to use a SWOT or PEST analysis to assist your work (*see Question 48*).
- Use the plan as a means of communicating to the members of your team, project sponsors and other stakeholders – telling them what you intend to do, when you will do it and how you will tackle tasks.
- Ensure that every member of the team signs off on the finalised plan, targets and timescale.

QUESTIONS TO ASK YOURSELF

- Do I spend too much/little time planning?
- Who can I ask to review the completed plan?

QUESTION 36   HOW DO I CALCULATE THE LENGTH OF A PROJECT?

Why it's important: There are two questions that everyone asks a project manager: 'What's the project about?' and 'When are you going to finish?' You must be able to answer both questions.

You've probably seen Gantt charts in the past. If not, Google them to see the very wide range of uses that they can be put to. You'll probably be pleased to know that it's not necessary for you to be an expert in the production of Gantt charts, as there are computer programs available that you or a member of your team, probably the monitor (*see Question 33*), can use. All you need to know are the principles that underpin Gantt charts.

Below is a simple example of a Gantt chart, which illustrates the stages in a small computer project.

Activity	Activity	Start week	End week	Duration: weeks
Meet with project sponsors and agree remit, resources and timetable	1	1	1	1
Identify, recruit and brief project team	2	2	3	2
Define and plan project with team	3	4	5	2
System design and programming	4	6	13	8
Select and order new hardware	5	5	5	1
Train staff	6	8	16	9
Install and test new hardware	7	10	11	2
Test system	8	14	16	3
Go live	9	17		

Activity	Week																
	1	2	3	4	5	6	7	8	9	10	11	12	13	14	15	16	17
1	█																
2		█	█														
3				█	█												
4						█	█	█	█	█	█	█	█				
5						█											
6								█	█	█	█	█	█	█	█	█	
7										█	█						
8														█	█	█	
9																	█

The chart shows that the project will take 16 weeks to complete and the system will 'Go live' during week 17. (To monitor progress against projection *see Question 39*.)

WHAT TO DO

- A Gantt chart can be used to help plan, manage and control projects. Draw one up as part of your planning process.
- Update the chart as the project timings are firmed up.
- Start by breaking the project down into its constituent tasks/targets (*see Question 39*).
- Attach to each task/target a start date and a deadline for its completion.
- Place each task/target in the order in which it must be started and show the duration and end date on the chart.

QUESTIONS TO ASK YOURSELF

- How committed to the deadlines are my project team?
- How confident am I that the estimates for each activity are achievable? Do I need to include a contingency of, say, two weeks?

QUESTION 37 **HOW CAN I MINIMISE THE RISKS ASSOCIATED WITH MY PROJECT?**

Why it's important: There are risks associated with everything you do. They can't be eliminated, but you can try to minimise the effect they might have on your project.

All plans are concerned with the future and therefore they contain within them potential risks because you are dealing with uncertainty and the unknown. Your job as project manager is to manage/minimise those risks and to take quick effective action if a risk evolves into a problem.

You can think of a risk in terms of the 'How likely is it to happen?' and 'If it does happen, how great will the impact be?'

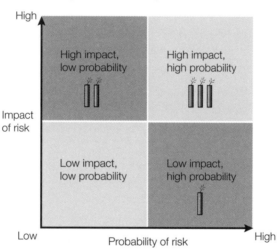

The areas of the project that you'll need to assess for risk are:

- All activities along the timeline that could pose a threat to costs, timescale or completion.
- The individual components of the project, including people, equipment and resources.
- Potential problems with suppliers.
- Changes within the organisation that might impact on the project.
- External events, such as changes in the market, financing, or government funding/tax regulations.
- At an interface between systems, departments or processes.

To deal with risk, you need a plan.

STRATEGIES TO USE IN A RISK CONTAINMENT PLAN:
Risk transfer: Move the risk from the team to external experts; for example, contract out the supply of say hardware or bespoke software.
Risk deferral: Change the order in which some activities are completed; for example, if some aspects of the project have yet to be confirmed, delay working on them until agreement has been reached (this will reduce the need for reworking).
Risk reduction: Either reduce the possibility that the risk will occur or lesson its impact if it should occur; for example, temporarily increase the number of people working on the project to meet potential bottlenecks.
Risk avoidance: Eliminate the possibility of the risk occurring; for example, use alternative resources or technologies.
Risk acceptance: Recognise that sometimes there's not a lot you can do other than accept the risk and ensure that contingency plans are in place.

WHAT TO DO

- As part of the planning process undertake an initial risk assessment. Work through your plan and ask such questions as:
  - What could happen that would affect the project?
  - What are the chances of this happening?
  - If it occurs, what effect will it have on the project?
  - What can we do to stop it happening?
  - What can we do to minimise the impact of the event should it occur?
- Use SWOT and PEST analysis (*see Question 48*) to identify the likelihood of an event occurring and its impact on the project.
- Focus your thinking on those risks that are high impact events that are most likely to occur. Develop a contingency plan for such events. The plan should only identify the main features of any actions you will take. The detail can be added if the worst happens.
- Allocate responsibility for monitoring each significant risk to an individual member of the team.

QUESTIONS TO ASK YOURSELF

- What's my attitude to risk? Am I a risk taker or a cautious Jo/Joe?
- How is my attitude to risk reflected in my planning for the project?

QUESTION 38 **HOW CAN I DELIVER THE MOST VALUABLE PARTS OF THE PROJECT AHEAD OF SCHEDULE?**

Why it's important: Self-protection. If you can't deliver everything on time, make sure you deliver the most important elements of a working project.

Have you ever wondered why so many public sector computer projects fail? It's not because the public sector lacks committed, well-trained professionals (as some tabloids would have you believe). The basic problem is hubris. The provision of public services is a complex operation, made more complicated by the number of clients that access each service. What this means is that just about every combination of events/ circumstances that could happen will happen. So staff try to design a system that will meet every eventuality. This makes for hugely complicated systems. But does every possible combination of events really have to be met? No, it doesn't.

Using the Pareto principle of the important few and the unimportant many, it's quite feasible to identify in any project (not just computer projects) the 80 per cent of the project that can be up and running while only consuming 20 per cent of the time and money set aside for the project. The remaining 20 per cent of the project requirements – the fiddly bits, which will consume the remaining 80 per cent of time available – can be added later (*see Question 7*).

WHAT TO DO

■ Within any project there are deliverables/components that are essential and those that are desirable. The essential deliverables are those which if met would deliver a basic working system, process or change. You need to identify these essential components. This should be done as part of project planning.

■ Think of these essential elements as the skeleton upon which the rest of the project can be hung or attached to.

■ Base your project plan on the delivery of the essential components first. The successful delivery of these components will give you 80 per cent of the project for 20 per cent of the cost and within 20 per cent of the timescale. Knowing that you have a basic working system/ process will take the pressure off you and your team and give you time to test and enhance the basic system and add the non-essential flourishes that will complete the project.

■ Just because you have a 'skeleton service' up and running early doesn't mean that you can relax in terms of monitoring and controlling the delivery of the rest of the project. You still have to complete the full project on time and to budget – even if the pressure is off to some extent. So stay focused.

■ If your TRAP analysis (*see Question 35*) shows that you don't have the resources to do the full job, and you are unable to renegotiate the project funding or delivery date, deliver the skeleton project as a priority and follow that up with as many non-essential features as the budget will allow. Tell the project board what you're doing.

QUESTIONS TO ASK YOURSELF

■ Who can help me identify the 80 per cent of the project that will enable me to deliver a working skeleton project?

■ What do I need to do to keep staff focused after we've delivered the skeleton project?

HOW DO I KEEP THE PROJECT ON TIME AND WITHIN BUDGET?

Why it's important: Your reputation depends not only on delivering the goods but doing so on time and to budget.

In Question 32 we saw that two primary responsibilities of any project manager were to deliver the project on time and under budget. To achieve this, a project manager needs to:

- Plan the project carefully with the help of their team (*see Question 35*), including the delivery dates for tasks and milestones.
- Regularly monitor actual performance against both the project plan and budget, and take corrective action when required (*see tables below*).

When defining the tasks, deadlines and milestones, it is helpful to use SMART targets:

SMART TARGETS ARE:
Specific: Clear and unambiguous.
Measurable: Have criteria against which success can be measured.
Achievable: Doable by a good employee.
Realistic: Realistic given the time and resources available for completion.
Timed: Have a deadline for completion.

WHAT TO DO

- Specify a date for the achievement of each task and milestone.
- Nominate a named individual to be responsible for the completion of each task, target and milestone.
- Use the SMART criteria to write a set of robust and realistic targets.
- Hold weekly monitoring meetings (*see Question 31*) and devise a simple reporting system that will enable you to monitor progress. For example:

Task	Performance to 1/4/XX	Notes	Comments and action required
Retrain 20% of staff by 20/4/XX. All staff to be trained by 30/6/XX	20%	Remaining 80% will be trained by 16/6/XX	None. We are ahead of target
Receive delivery of machines by 10/4/XX		Delay of one month reported by suppliers	PM to speak to Director X and ask Director to threaten withdrawal of contract unless original delivery date met

- To monitor the actual expenditure against budget you need to devise a budget for the entire project (*see Questions 60 and 61*). While this document must be your own budget, work with your accountant if at all possible. They can bring a lot of expertise to this area of work.
- Allocate responsibility for each individual account to a member of the team.
- At the end of each month table a budget/actual report at the team meetings (*see Question 31*). For example, this will enable you to monitor progress and take prompt action if required. Don't hold a weekly budget meeting as this just adds to the admin and is not required. Hold this team meeting before you report to the project sponsors' meeting at the end of the month. That way you can provide the sponsors with the most up-to-date information available and details of any actions you've taken.

Account	A/C code	Budget to date	Actual to date	Variance (Favourable/ Unfavourable)	Action
Project salaries	Sal/001	4,600	4,500	F/100	None required
Project overtime	Sal/002	1,200	3,000	U/1,800	Change to order of work is responsible for the apparent overspend. This will be corrected by 31/4/XX

QUESTIONS TO ASK YOURSELF

- Who is going to be responsible for the production of the weekly progress report?
- Who is going to be responsible for the production of the monthly budget report?

QUESTION 40 # HOW CAN I IMPROVE MY TEAM'S EFFECTIVENESS?

Why it's important: Managers are judged on how effective they and their team are in terms of meeting their targets and objectives.

You will see in Question 65 that value for money is concerned with economy, efficiency and effectiveness. Of these, effectiveness is the most important factor because you can be as economic and efficient as you like but if you fail to achieve your objectives then what's the point? That's what effectiveness is about – achieving what you set out to achieve. Whether you are managing a project or working with your regular staff, you can only achieve your objectives through the efforts of your team.

Douglas McGregor identified the following features of effective teams.

GOOD TEAMS:
Operate in an informal and relaxed manner/atmosphere.
Regularly discuss issues, with all members of the team making contributions.
Are clear about their objectives and committed to achieving them.
Listen to the views of colleagues and communicate effectively.
Resolve conflict within the team, without outside interference.
Aim to find consensus when making decisions.
Are comprised of people who are happy to speak their mind and express their ideas and opinions openly.
Share responsibility for team leadership.
Constantly reflect upon their performance and actions.

To improve team effectiveness, you need to aim for the above and eliminate the factors that make a failing team (*see Question 26*).

WHAT TO DO

- As a manager your aim is to ensure that your team has as many features of a good team as possible.

- Start with your selection of team members (*see Questions 16 and 33*). Make sure that you only select committed, enthusiastic and motivated people who want to get the job done. It's hard to motivate those who can't or won't motivate themselves.

- Brief each member of the team individually and the team collectively as soon after the formation of the team as possible. Make it clear what you expect from each person.

- Lead by example and demonstrate in your actions how you want every team member to act. For example, you can't expect the team to accept criticism if you argue with anyone who dares to say that you are less than perfect.

- Use your daily interaction with team members, team meetings and discussions with individuals to monitor how the team is feeling and acting. Tackle any problems identified.

- Check with people outside the team how members of the group are perceived, behaving and interacting with the wider organisation. Are team members positive and helpful, or carriers of scepticism and doom?

- Meet with your team worker (*see Question 33*) regularly. Go through the features of ineffective teams with them and ask if they have seen any of the signs that distinguish good and bad teams.

- Take appropriate action to remedy specific problems. For example, if there is unresolved conflict within the team, either speak with the individuals involved and tell them to sort it out themselves, or get involved and act as mediator (*see Question 23*).

QUESTIONS TO ASK YOURSELF

- Am I the problem? Do I dominate the team?
- Are there any individuals within the team who cause unrest/resentment? If so, what can I do?

QUESTION 41 # HOW DO I DEAL WITH REQUESTS TO AMEND A PROJECT AFTER IT HAS STARTED?

Why it's important: Saying no to those in authority isn't easy, but sometimes it's essential.

Projects often start off as tight little packages with a single clear aim and everyone pulling in the same direction. Unfortunately, this state of affairs rarely lasts long. Outsiders suddenly see an opportunity to solve one of their problems by enlarging the project and changing its aims. Accepting changes leads to additional work and missed deadlines. This is a recipe for disaster and something that every project manager must resist.

Even apparently small and insignificant requests will require changes to the project plan and timescale. This diverts resources from the main aim of the project. Do this often enough and suddenly the team is so busy dealing with unplanned changes that it ends up ignoring its central purpose.

WHAT TO DO

- Start as you intend to go on. Reach agreement with the sponsors of the project that they will protect you and the team from outside pressure. In particular, identify one or two sponsors on whom you can depend to support you in resisting all spurious requests for change. Usually these will be the ones who have the most to lose if the project is delayed or fails.

- Get your response in first. Announce to everyone who is willing, or even unwilling, to listen that changes to the basic project will not be entertained.

- Establish a system for dealing with requests for changes. Insist that all requests be directed to you in the first instance. This will stop people selling the change to project sponsors before you've even seen it.

- You will be able to squash many requests by speaking to whoever requested the change and explaining the position. Where this is not possible and you are being pressured to accept a change by another manager, write a short report to them and copy it to the project sponsors. Detail the additional cost of the change, the resources that would have to be diverted from existing work to implement the change, and the effect that it would have on the project's final completion date. Place the request on the agenda for your monthly meeting with sponsors (*see Question 31*).

- Devise and rehearse a standard response to requests for change.

- If you know that you are 'too eager to please', take steps to become more assertive.

- If the flow of requests becomes substantial, negotiate a Phase 2 to the current project with your sponsors. Thereafter, as requests for changes come in, both you and your sponsors can decline the request but assure the person that it will be considered as part of the Phase 2 project.

QUESTIONS TO ASK YOURSELF

- Do I need to be more assertive with people who are senior to me in the organisation?

- How good am I at negotiating win/win solutions (*see Question 55*)?

QUESTION 42 # WHAT CAN I DO IF THE PROJECT STARTS TO GO WRONG?

Why it's important: There is always a stage in any project where there is the potential for it to go pear-shaped. How you react to this will determine if the project succeeds or fails.

On the basis that prevention is better than cure, you should try to stop problems arising rather than try to solve them as they arise.

A PROJECT IS MOST LIKELY TO GO WRONG WHERE THERE IS/HAS BEEN:

Poor specification of the project, with overly ambitious outcomes and/or unclear measures of success.

An unrealistic/overly optimistic timescale.

Poor leadership of the project team.

Inclusion of people in the project team who have neither the required skills nor experience.

Insufficient oversight and/or support by senior management.

Failure to manage user expectations.

Failure to adequately monitor the project and seek additional help and support at a stage early enough to take effective remedial action.

Project failures are also more likely at any interface between systems, departments, organisations or different project teams. This is a particularly high risk when dealing with computer systems.

WHAT TO DO

- Working with the project team, identify the problems that could arise under each of the areas listed above, and list also their warning signs (*see Question 37*).

- Develop a flexible contingency plan for dealing with each problem. Don't invest a huge amount of time in this. Just outline in broad terms the response you would take if the risk becomes real. You can add details as and when the warning bells ring.

- Allocate responsibility for monitoring each potential problem to an individual member of the project team (*see Question 39*).

- Take action immediately the problem shows itself. Don't prevaricate and hope that it will go away. It won't. If you need to replace someone in the team, do it quickly. Brief the newcomer fully so that they can hit the floor running. If you find yourself out of your depth, ask for help/advice.

- Don't accept unrealistic deadlines from management. Remember that Confucius wasn't keen on self-sacrificing heroes.

- When drawing up your project plan consider alternative ways of achieving the same objective. Record these unused alternatives – they might just save your job and the project when problems arise.

- Don't be afraid to take a step back and change your project plan if it enables you to sidestep a possible problem or delay. Be flexible – but always keep the end in mind.

QUESTIONS TO ASK YOURSELF

- What support from the project sponsors can I call upon if problems arise?

- Is there an experienced project manager in the organisation that I can talk to?

QUESTION 43   # HOW CAN I PASS ON WHAT I'VE LEARNT TO OTHER PROJECT MANAGERS?

Why it's important: Only a fool makes the same mistake time and again.

An ancient sage (not Confucius!) once said 'It's difficult to remember that your job was to drain the swamp when the crocodiles are biting your bum'. The same is true about learning lessons from projects. At the end of a successful project it's easy to forget what you have learnt from the project, as you are too busy trying to get through the backlog of work that has accumulated while you've been away from your 'day job'. Yes, you'll remember the big things – like how computer specialists will always deliver the system they think you need and not the one you asked for (unless you make it very clear to them that they don't run the show). But the little things are more easily forgotten. Yet these are the things that when combined can improve the management of future projects. You need a strategy for capturing this information.

WHAT TO DO

- If possible, spare a few minutes at the end of the day to record briefly in your reflective diary any lessons learnt. Include both positive and negative experiences.

- At the end of each weekly progress meeting, ask the team members if they have any items they would like recorded under 'lessons learnt' in the action notes that will be issued at the end of the meeting. This will only take a few minutes and has the added advantage of spreading good ideas and practice during the life of the current project, as well as informing future projects.

- After each monthly meeting with the project sponsors, record anything that you think might help you and other project managers deal more effectively with senior management.

- Once the project has been completed, make a list of all the ideas recorded in your reflective diary, the project team meetings' action notes and the minutes of the monthly sponsors' meetings.

- Include a list of lessons learnt in your final report to the project sponsors and senior management. They may or may not pick up on them or disseminate them around the organisation but at least you will have a very valuable resource for the next project you manage.

- When you are given the next project, do your homework. Review what you learnt from the previous project and see how you can avoid some of the mistakes you and your team made. Just as importantly, think about how you can expand on and run with the good things that you and your team did.

QUESTIONS TO ASK YOURSELF

- How good am I at learning from my mistakes?
- How can I become better at learning from experience?

KEY MESSAGES TO TAKE FROM THIS SECTION

- Identify the aims of the project and summarise them in a single sentence.
- Use the TRAP analysis to assess if you have any chance of success. If you have little or no chance of success, then renegotiate the terms of the project with sponsors.
- Do all you can to have the final say in who will be included in the project team.
- Learn to say no – especially to your bosses.
- Plan the project on the basis of delivering a skeleton working project before adding the fiddly bits.
- Keep reports and meetings to a minimum.
- Take corrective action as soon as you spot the potential for a problem. Similarly, be prepared to run with unexpected positives that arrive, and try to build on them.

SECTION 4

NAVIGATING THE WIDER ORGANISATION

When the Master arrives in a state, he invariably gets to know about its government. [He collects information] through being cordial, good, respectful, frugal and deferential. The way the Master seeks it is, perhaps, different from the way that other men seek it.
Confucius, *Analects* 1.10

In his errors a man is true to type. Observe the errors and you will know the man.
Confucius, *Analects* 4.7

INTRODUCTION

In Section 1 I suggested that the one thing managers lack is time. So is it any wonder that many managers end up ignoring what is going on in the wider organisation and world as they struggle with the problems of their own departments and teams on a daily basis? This is understandable, but it's still a mistake. Your future success is dependent on the organisation continuing to be successful, and on the actions of those senior to you.

You need to understand what makes your organisation tick; who the key players are; where it's heading as an organisation; what key threats and opportunities it faces. You need to become as near indispensable as you can to those who make decisions about your future. And, if things do go wrong, you need to identify the signs of impending organisational failure early enough to abandon the sinking ship before it drags you down with it.

Study the organisation and the people within it. Observe key players. Examine how they respond to both personal successes and failures. The qualities that leaders require when the business is under attack – like calmness, tenacity, an ability to work harder and longer than anyone else and indefectibility – aren't always found in the charming, charismatic, media-friendly managers who are so admired when things are going their way. Personally, I've always judged the worth of managers on the basis of 'Who would I want fighting with me in the trenches if the worst happens?'

Finally, remember that it is not just your boss that you have to impress in order to progress. If your boss leaves, it will be their boss who is likely to interview possible replacements. So, always look to impress those who are one or two levels above your boss.

QUESTION 44 WHAT IS THE ORGANISATION'S CULTURE AND DOES IT SUIT ME?

Why it's important: To be an effective manager you have to understand and be able to work with the dominant organisational culture.

Organisational culture is ephemeral and difficult to define. Terrence Deal and Allan Kennedy defined it as 'The way we do things around here' and, by extension, 'What we value around here'. If as a manager you act contrary to the accepted norms of the organisation, you'll find your career going nowhere unless you have been specifically employed to shake the organisation up and change its culture.

A quick and easy way to identify your organisation's culture is to use Charles Handy's four cultures model to analyse your organisation's culture and your own preference. These four cultures are:

Club (or power)	Role (or bureaucratic)
This is where a single person or small elite is all powerful. Think of firms established, run and owned by a single person. What they say goes, and people try to act in a way that they think the person or group would approve of. Decisions are based on who holds the most power.	This organisation's structure is hierarchical and staff are expected to work to their job description and follow laid-down rules and procedures. A typical example is the civil service, but the reality is that many large commercial organisations are also highly bureaucratic.
Task (or team)	**Existential (or individual)**
This culture values team working. It's often found in schools, universities, research establishments and organisations involved in creative work. It can include any organisation where success is dependent upon bringing together the disparate skills and knowledge of a group of people to solve a problem.	This culture is based on individuals who see the organisation as existing merely to enable them to exercise their skills and expertise. Think of firms of architects and barristers, which are created to serve the needs of the professionals in them.

The precise mix and relative strength of these cultures produce an organisation's unique culture. As can be seen from the following table, it's normal for one or two cultures to dominate.

Organisation	Club %	Bureaucratic %	Team %	Individual %
Organisation 1	60	25	10	5
Organisation 2	20	70	8	2

WHAT TO DO

- Complete Handy's organisational culture questionnaire (available online, or see his book *Understanding Organizations*). The results will identify your organisation's culture and the one that you are most suited to.

- If your organisation's culture matches your preference, you'll have few problems. However, if you work in a power culture but prefer a mix of bureaucracy and team culture, you will find it hard to adapt. If you can't adapt, you may have to leave.

- Identify a successful manager in the organisation and study how they behave and the management approach they adopt. If appropriate, use them as a role model.

- Once you know how things are done in your organisation, keep this in mind when taking action, making changes or taking decisions. Very often what you want to do will be non-contentious, but if you implement an idea in a way that clashes with the organisation's cultural norms you will find yourself fighting an uphill battle. So think carefully about what approach/tactics you will use.

QUESTIONS TO ASK YOURSELF

- What is my organisation's dominant culture?
- Does my management style accord, or clash, with the organisation's dominant culture?

HOW DO I IDENTIFY THE KEY PEOPLE IN THE ORGANISATION WHO I NEED TO KEEP SWEET?

Why it's important: You want the key people in the organisation to know and respect you because it is they who control your future prospects.

Don't confuse position with power. In every organisation there are board members and executives who are respected and listened to and those who are side-lined and ignored. It is the powerful and influential people in your organisation who you need to keep sweet. In Question 3 seven sources of power were identified. These are:

- traditional authority
- legal rational authority
- charismatic power
- reward power
- coercive power
- expert power
- negative power.

The stars in your organisation will be the senior executives and senior managers who can utilise all the sources of power available to them and do so with a high level of expertise and skill. These are the people that you need to keep sweet.

WHAT TO DO

- There is one manager that you must always keep sweet – your own boss (*see Question 8*). If you don't, they can make your life miserable and block your progress.
- The second person you need to impress is your boss's boss. This is the person who will appoint a replacement for your boss when the times comes.
- Use your organisation chart to identify the possible key players (*see Question 50*).

■ Use conversations and meetings with colleagues and senior managers to identify the true key players from your list of possibles. These are the people who:

- have demonstrated skill in using all seven sources of power;
- are spoken about with either admiration or respect, especially by their 'enemies';
- have stories told about them and their exploits;
- are listened to in meetings or asked for their advice/views;
- have a track record of achievement;
- appear able to influence events and decisions in the organisation;
- are able to draw people to them;
- usually get their own way;
- run a department or team with a particularly good reputation;
- are seen as someone you don't want to cross;
- are able to use several sources of power effectively.

■ Find a way to make yourself known to as many of the key people as possible (*see Question 25*).

■ For those people with whom you come into contact regularly, identify ways in which you can influence their opinion of you (*see Question 8*).

■ On the basis that it is always better to be useful than to be liked by your bosses (*see Question 46*), find out what information or service they particularly value/need – and provide it. This makes you valuable to them and the job they do.

■ Support the views of key players and their ideas whenever you can. Don't oppose them in public – you'll only lose, and also make an enemy. Better to remain silent and raise your concerns with them in private if you have the opportunity.

QUESTIONS TO ASK YOURSELF

■ How good am I at networking?

■ How am I perceived by others in the organisation? Do I need to change that perception?

QUESTION 46 — HOW DO I SURVIVE ORGANISATIONAL POLITICS?

Why it's important: Whether you like it or not, organisational politics come with the job. So you need to know how to protect yourself.

The two major problems associated with organisational politics are that it distracts people from the real work of the organisation and that it has a habit of harming innocent bystanders. So, even if you have no interest in organisational politics, you need to know how to defend yourself against those who see you as no more than a pawn in their game of power.

To defend yourself you need to understand your enemy. The patron saint of most politicos is Machiavelli. Why? Because he provided them with a justification for acting ruthlessly by arguing that an act is virtuous if it achieves its aim. Such justification soothes what remains of their conscience.

MACHIAVELLIANS BELIEVE THAT:

People are dispensable once they have outlived their usefulness.

They must destroy totally any threat to their position before that threat has a chance to develop.

If they have recently been appointed to a new job they must consolidate their position by crushing completely any elements that remain loyal to the previous regime.

Anyone who has helped them achieve their position has to be eliminated. This is because by sacrificing a friend/colleague they will be feared. In addition, if that person is not dealt with then they may come to resent them and believe that the job should have been theirs.

It's better to be feared than loved, because love can wane and with it loyalty, whereas the fear of retribution grows with every ruthless act.

WHAT TO DO

- Machiavellians may be ruthless but they are not stupid. They know they need the help of other people to achieve their aims. Therefore it's essential that you remain useful to them (*see Question 8*). As long as they need you, you're safe.

- Never give politicos an excuse for thinking that you are, have been, or ever will be disloyal to them.

- If the Machiavellian colleague is newly appointed and you were part of the previous regime, make it clear that you're loyal to them. Never start a sentence with 'Well previously, we used to ...'. It's a recipe for transfer to whatever counts as a gulag in your organisation.

- Never help a Machiavellian into a position of power. You may as well paint a target on your back and wait for elimination. Machiavellians know that previous allies often become disillusioned and believe that they should have taken the job for themselves.

- Recognise that Machiavellians will sacrifice you at any time if they think it will benefit them. Therefore remain relevant to their plans and useful to them in what you deliver. Remind them from time to time just how useful you are.

- Don't take sides in any dispute between senior managers or factions. Keep your own counsel and let people interpret your silence however they wish. Usually people take silence as a sign that you agree with them.

- Remember, knowledge is power. Find some sensitive information that you can use as an insurance policy.

QUESTIONS TO ASK YOURSELF

- What is my strategy for dealing with Machiavellian managers?
- What sensitive information do I have about the power brokers in the organisation that might protect me?

HOW DO I PLAY THE GAME OF ORGANISATIONAL POLITICS AND WIN?

Why it's important: If you are going to play, you need to know what you're doing.

I'm not suggesting that you should become involved in organisational politics. Personally I think it reduces your effectiveness as a manager. Only you can decide if you are willing to accept the risks involved. But if you are determined to play, remember that it can be a deadly affair, and to be successful requires the right mentality.

To play the game successfully you'll need to learn a lot more about the dark arts than the strategies I've listed below. Check out the recommended reading at the end of the book.

WHAT TO DO

- Keep control of your emotions. Never lose your temper. Don't react to provocation. Clock the 'insult' and wait for the right moment to strike. Patience is essential. Play the long game.
- Always seek to be underestimated by your opponents. Act like an innocent fool to catch a fool. President Reagan, who was constantly underestimated by his opponents, was a master at this.
- There are only so many people you can fight at one time. If possible, try to win support by using constructive transactions before reverting to coercive transactions (*see Question 28*).
- Recognise that only you can keep your secrets. Never reveal what you're thinking or what your intentions are, especially to friends.
- If possible, use someone else to front any attack you make. That way, if it fails, you can deny all knowledge of it.
- Choose your moment to attack. Attack when your quarry is at its most vulnerable. Often this is when they feel most secure – perhaps after a victory. Then attack with maximum force. Show no mercy and destroy them completely. If you don't, they will regroup and seek revenge.
- Be very cautious about entering into any alliance with another player. If you do, you have to be willing to destroy them in due course, since

there is no way that they are ever going to trust you after you've taken out your joint target.

■ Don't become isolated. Knowledge is power. Get out and collect as much information from staff, colleagues and senior managers as you can and then guard it jealously (*see Question 48*).

■ Before you ask someone to help you, discover what their strengths and weaknesses are and exploit these during your discussions with them.

■ Identify who the important players are in the organisation (*see Question 45*) and court their support. Never make an enemy of these people until you have the resources and power to fight them. Run away if you have to, and fight only when you are ready.

■ Discover the weakness of every person you come into contact with. When necessary, use that weakness to get your own way. For example, if they're proud of their intellect, treat them like an idiot. They'll be so annoyed they'll find it hard to think straight.

■ Never follow a great manager into a job. You'll be constantly compared to them. Better to let someone else have the job and when they fail or leave then you take the post.

■ If you are opposed by a group, identify the leader and attack them. Once they have been defeated the followers will scatter.

QUESTIONS TO ASK YOURSELF

■ Do I really want to play the politics game?
■ Have I got the right personality to be successful?

QUESTION 48 HOW DO I KEEP ABREAST OF CHANGES THAT MIGHT AFFECT ME AND MY ORGANISATION?

Why it's important: Information is power. It's also vital for making good decisions.

To be an effective manager you need to keep abreast of what's going on outside your domain that might affect you and the organisation. In the 'What to do' section below I suggest a number of information sources that you should access regularly, but here I'd like to remind you of the value of undertaking a regular PEST and SWOT analysis at least annually and preferably six monthly.

The purpose of a SWOT exercise is to identify the strengths, weaknesses, opportunities and threats that face the organisation. While it is often assumed that SWOT is concerned only with internal factors, it also throws up many external factors that might be missed by a PEST analysis, because it looks at issues other than political, economic, social and technological.

FACTORS TO CONSIDER IN A SWOT ANALYSIS:

Strengths and weaknesses, including the organisation's financial strength, product range, market share, access to skilled workers, ability to react to change, customer loyalty, and its relationship with institutional investors and its bank.

Opportunities and threats, including changes to the nature and composition of the competition, financial and economic conditions, barriers to new entrants, changes in customer demand, product range, market share and the impact of technology.

When circumstances change, strengths and opportunities can become a weakness or threat or vice versa.

FACTORS TO CONSIDER IN A PEST ANALYSIS:

Political factors, including government and EU policies, existing and pending regulations and legislation, and changes in government policy following elections.

Economic changes/problems in local, national, eurozone and world markets, including economic growth forecasts, exchange rates and the level of unemployment.

Social trends, including the growth of online shopping and business, an ageing population, and changes in social attitudes.

Technological trends, including new discoveries and manufacturing processes (for example, the potential of 3D printing to allow customers to 'build' their own objects), the ever-increasing speed of technological transfer, and its impact on lead times and production cycles.

WHAT TO DO

FOR BOTH A SWOT AND PEST ANALYSIS

- Decide if you are going to conduct a solo analysis or use a small team. The team approach will be more effective.
- Define precisely the purpose of the exercise before you start, and share with the team some examples of what to look for. Concentrate on issues that could impact on the organisation in the short to medium term. Anything longer and you're into guess work.
- Use brainstorming and any information that the organisation has already collected to identify issues.
- Give each person a pack of post-it notes and ask them to list as many possible factors as possible.
- Using the wall as your notice board, arrange all the ideas under the relevant factor and summarise the ideas generated.
- Evaluate each factor in terms of how likely it is to happen and what its effect will be on the organisation if it does. Use quantitative and qualitative data and personal insights (tacit knowledge) to evaluate the issues (*see Questions 5 and 75*).
- If there is more than a 30 per cent chance of the event happening, and it would have a significant effect on the organisation, it's worth analysing further (*see Question 37*).
- Briefly outline a strategy for dealing with all those threats that have

breached the 30 per cent level. You probably don't have the time or resources to consider events with a probability of less than 30 per cent.

■ Make a note in your reflective diary of anything of interest that you pick up and/or take time to reflect on what you've identified before taking action.

■ Remember that a strength is only a strength if it gives you a competitive advantage over your competitors. So you need to ask yourself if your staff really are better trained and more committed than the opposition's staff before you list it as a strength.

FOR A SWOT ANALYSIS

■ To ensure that you have the raw material to work with in your SWOT analysis, gather as much information as you can. Use information gained from your PEST analysis as appropriate.

■ Keep your eyes and ears open. Use every conversation you have and meeting you attend as an opportunity to pick up information.

■ Always be willing to listen to those who hold unpopular views or views contrary to the organisation's official message or received wisdom. Why? Because every new idea starts with just one person and was downright stupid until the majority of people took it on board.

■ Use MBWA (management by walking about) (*see Question 50*) as a way to collect information. Always define a purpose for your walk about in advance, but be willing to abandon it if something really interesting comes up. Don't interrogate people – simply engage them in conversation and use non-threatening, open questions to draw them out. People love being asked for their opinion and most of us can bore for Britain if we're given the chance. Listen actively to what people say and use prompts such as 'I've never thought of that …', 'Can you tell me more about …'

■ When you get back to the office make a note in your reflective diary of any issue raised that you want to explore further. Ask yourself: does any of this link to other pieces of data that I already have?

■ Learn about parts of the organisation that you have nothing to do with. Only when you understand the organisation as a single entity can you plan to meet the threats and opportunities it faces.

FOR A PEST ANALYSIS

- Subscribe to a good broadsheet newspaper and read it. The *Financial Times* is the best paper for business but takes an age to read. Settle for one of the other broadsheets.

- Subscribe to any trade magazines that are relevant to your organisation. They will keep you informed of the major changes and innovations in your part of the universe.

- Identify a selection of websites and blogs – not too many – that cover your business sector and access them regularly.

- Check with your marketing team to see if they receive a monthly digest of articles that have appeared in the press or online that mention your organisation.

- Build a network of contacts with people who work in your sector. Trade and professional gatherings are a good place to start.

- Check the radio and TV listings for programmes that deal with management and business. I particularly recommend *The Bottom Line* on BBC Radio 4.

- Attend an interview at least once a year, even if you aren't looking for a new job – you need to keep in practice.

QUESTIONS TO ASK YOURSELF

- What are the major threats that face the organisation/my team?
- Do I have a strategy for dealing with such threats?

QUESTION 49 # WHAT ARE THE SIGNS THAT THE ORGANISATION IS IN DANGER OF COLLAPSE?

Why it's important: Self-preservation!

There are a number of signs that warn of an organisation's impending collapse. Unfortunately, not everyone in the organisation has access to the strategic and financial information that signals such danger. But there are other signs you can look out for.

SIGNS THAT AN ORGANISATION IS IN DANGER OF COLLAPSE:

An inability by senior executives and the board to confront reality and make the changes required; instead, they talk of grandiose schemes that will never happen. (I left one organisation when the chief executive suggested we hire a plane and take every manager in the organisation to Tenerife for a planning and bonding weekend when he knew that cash flow was tight and profits down.)

Difficulty in getting a straight answer to a straight question from bosses about the organisation and its future.

Signs that the chairman's ego is running out of control (for example, looking to raise their profile by indulging in a vanity project such as buying a football club).

A high turnover in board members, or directors unloading their shares as if it was October 1929 on Wall Street.

Delays in the annual accounts being published, refusal of the auditors to sign off the accounts, or – worse still – the resignation of the auditors.

The refusal of management to listen to the finance director, and downplaying the importance of financial information (phrases like 'Financial problems are temporary. You've got to see the big picture.' are typical).

Underworked front-line staff, with orders declining and customers taking longer to pay.

Difficulty in obtaining supplies, or suppliers complaining that they can't get paid on time.

Decisions being taken without any sign of a long-term strategy.

WHAT TO DO

- Prepare in advance for that rainy day that affects most careers at some time. Build up a network of contacts both within and outside your organisation that might be useful if you find yourself out of work.

- Humphrey Bogart was a great film actor but not the most pleasant person. He wanted to be able to tell any film executive what they could do if they crossed him. So he built up what he called his 'F*** you fund'. You need a similar fund. Work out your monthly committed and essential expenditure and save between three and six times that amount. More if possible. That way you will always have some cash to fall back on.

- Keep yourself marketable. Even if you have no intention of changing jobs, attend at least one interview a year. You need to be match-fit to pass an interview, so don't get out of practice. If you're faced with your first interview in five years it can be a daunting experience – especially if you really need the job.

- Constantly upgrade your professional skills and knowledge. Your greatest asset is yourself. So invest in your own professional development.

- Monitor the financial press/websites for stories about your organisation.

- If you spot three or more of the above signs, start digging your escape tunnel. Apply for jobs immediately.

- If you find it impossible to move, hang on to the bitter end and check out what redundancy payments you are due from the organisation or government.

QUESTIONS TO ASK YOURSELF

- Who in the organisation can I trust to tell me what's really going on?
- How good is my external network of business contacts?

WHERE DO I FIND AN ORGANISATION CHART THAT SHOWS HOW THINGS REALLY WORK?

Why it's important: You need an overview of the organisation and where you fit into it, a chart that shows where the real power and authority reside in the organisation.

This entry is primarily for aspiring, new and junior managers, but all managers need reminding of the words of Machiavelli – that unsuccessful leaders nearly always deal with the reality they wished existed rather than the reality that confronts them?

You already know that the organisation chart pinned to your wall was out of date before it was published, but that doesn't mean all charts are useless. You need a chart that depicts both the formal and informal relationships that exist between departments and individuals in the organisation. Unless you can plug into the informal network of relationships and power centres, you'll struggle to be effective.

FOUR TYPES OF ORGANISATIONAL CHARTS:

The official organisation chart for public consumption. This is the one given to new staff and shareholders and is an outdated and over-simplified picture of a complex reality.

The chart that individuals update as changes occur and which they keep in their desk. Unfortunately, they only record the changes that are formally announced and which relate directly to them. These individuals often mistakenly believe that their chart is a realistic representation of the organisational reality.

The unwritten and unofficial chart that experienced staff keep in their head and which enables them to short-cut the organisation's formal structure and get things done through a network of friends and contacts. This chart is part of the person's tacit knowledge (*see Question 5*) and these people would find it impossible to describe it fully to another person.

The chart that depicts the true reality of the organisation but which is impossible to draw as all managers and staff only have partial knowledge of the organisation and their role in it.

It's the third chart that you need. Your own unique chart that will enable you to identify your position in the organisation, your relationships with other key individuals and managers, and shifts in power between individuals and departments. This knowledge will enable you to side-step some of the worst bureaucratic roadblocks, get things done, and not fall foul of power plays by other managers and individuals (*see Question 46*). However, useful as this chart is, you must remember that it still only provides you with a partial picture of the real organisation.

WHAT TO DO

- Acquire a copy of the firm's published organisation chart and study it.
- Get out of your office on a regular basis and undertake a bit of management by walking about (MBWA). Before you start, identify the purpose of each walk; for example, how do staff feel about the latest restructuring?
- Your aim is to discover what people feel and think about what's going on, and how it has affected their relationships with other staff and departments.
- Listen to what people say. Don't tell them what you think. Use your eyes to see how different sections, teams and departments behave and interact. Keep your mouth shut and your ears open.
- In meetings with your boss and/or other managers, clock what is going on. Which people/departments have formed alliances? Which manager is at war with a colleague, and why? Who is listened to in meetings? Where does the power reside in the room? What alliances and enmities are on show?
- When talking with other managers informally, listen to what they say. Don't sit there waiting to jump in with your own brilliant opinion. You learn nothing from listening to your own voice.
- Either make a mental note or jot down any relevant data that you have collected from walks and meetings, and use them to revise your organisation chart.
- Rather than draw a conventional organisation chart, use a mind map to represent the reality of relationships within your organisation. This will allow for multiple linkages between departments and individuals and give a much better image of the complexity that you are trying to capture.

- Use continuous lines for formal relations between departments and important individuals, and dotted lines to show informal relationships. You could colour code your chart to show where power lies and where it flows to. The darker the colour, the stronger the power. But remember, no matter how detailed your mind map is, it's only a pale shadow of the complex picture that resides in your head as tacit knowledge. However, working on your mind map will both feed and reveal that knowledge.

QUESTIONS TO ASK YOURSELF

- Who do people listen to in the organisation?
- Who socialises with whom? What's their real relationship?

KEY MESSAGES TO TAKE FROM THIS SECTION

- Know where you and your team fit into the organisation.
- Identify the organisation's culture and work with it.
- Identify the key people in your organisation who can affect your future, and become known to them.
- Identify and develop either a specialist skill, knowledge or service that makes you valuable to senior management.
- If you are going to become involved with organisational politics, learn more about it.
- Constantly monitor the strengths, weaknesses, opportunities and threats that face the organisation, and your department/team in particular.
- Always have an escape plan should the organisation fail.

SECTION 5

WORKING WITH CUSTOMERS AND SUPPLIERS

At court when speaking to Counsellors of lower rank he [Confucius] was affable; when speaking with Counsellors of upper rank, he was frank though respectful. In the presence of his Lord, his bearing, though respectful, was composed.
Confucius, *Analects* 10.2

INTRODUCTION

It would be a mistake to assume that this section only applies to those managers who deal with external customers and suppliers. The same principles apply when dealing with internal customers and suppliers. Unfortunately, too many managers fail to treat internal colleagues as they do outsiders. The result is that internal relationships are underdeveloped and strained. Just think of the improvements in economy, efficiency, effectiveness, staff co-operation and morale if those relationships were improved.

If you don't buy into my argument that improving internal relationships improves productivity and profits then think about it in purely selfish terms. Internal customers or suppliers may be stuck with a poor level of service from you. But they are in a much better position than any outsider to ruin your reputation if you constantly provide a poor level of service or treat them as a nuisance to be tolerated.

How you deal with customers and suppliers will determine the long-term success of your relationship with them. When dealing with either group, aim for what the management guru Stephen Covey called a win/win solution. This means that both parties come away from any deal feeling fully satisfied. This is a very different feeling to the situation where a compromise has been reached. In such instances neither party is fully satisfied (*see Question 23*).

To achieve a win/win you need to identify what the other person wants from the deal and find a way to give it to them while ensuring that you also obtain what you want. If you can do this consistently you'll enjoy strong relationships that are built on trust and mutual satisfaction. This means that when times are bad both customers and suppliers are more likely to be supportive towards you and your organisation.

Note: The term 'product' is used extensively in this section and relates to both manufactured goods and/or services. The advice given also applies to both in-house and external customers.

HOW DO I BUILD POSITIVE RELATIONSHIPS WITH MY CUSTOMERS AND MAKE THEM FEEL VALUED?

Why it's important: Business is about relationships, not just the sale of goods and services.

Peter Drucker argued that the purpose of every business was to create a customer. Once that's achieved it's necessary to retain and grow every customer. Without customers there are no profits.

Yet, despite Drucker's advice, one of the major reasons why customers switch suppliers is because they feel underappreciated and taken for granted. For example, how do you feel when only new customers are offered a great new deal on insurance, savings, mortgages or mobile phones from your current supplier?

To retain your existing customer base and add to it, you need to keep your customer more than satisfied or else they will walk. With some companies customers positively sprint when they get the chance.

WHAT TO DO

- Stay in touch with your customers. Communicate with them on a regular basis, even when you're not trying to sell them something. Use email, phone, newsletters and personal visits to build up your relationship. Invite them to special events. If you see an advert or a news item that might be of interest to them, send them a copy.

- Build trust. Always keep your word. Don't renege on a deal or a promise, even if it means you lose money. Give your best customers your best deals – don't exploit them. If you screw them over once, and they find out, you'll lose all the credibility that you have built up and probably their custom. Conversely, if you have a product that only meets 85 per cent of their needs, but know of one that meets 100 per cent, then tell them about it. Yes, you'll lose that sale but you've assured their future trust and custom big time.

- Be honest with customers. If there is a problem with, say, a delivery date, tell them. If you can't answer a question, don't invent an answer. Tell them you don't know but that you'll find out and get back to them.

- Listen to what your customers say. Open your ears and close your mouth and listen. Let them talk about their business, your products, your competitors' products and why they prefer yours. If you're really lucky they will tell you what products they wish you offered. This will help you to identify what their true needs are – not what you think they are – and can be a source of new business.

- Use feedback as a means of finding out how well your product or service meets the needs of customers. What's good about it? What's bad? What improvements would customers like to see? Don't be defensive about criticism. See it as an opportunity to identify both how to improve existing products and identify potential new products.

- Recognise customer loyalty by offering a range of rewards, including discounts, better payment terms, special deals and invitations to special events.

- In all dealings with customers keep brief notes and when you get the time write them up. That way you can build up a profile for each customer and spot developing trends.

QUESTIONS TO ASK YOURSELF

- Do I view my customers as valuable colleagues or a herd of cash cows?

- Do I know what annoys my customers most about dealing with my organisation?

WHAT'S THE BEST WAY TO RESPOND TO CUSTOMER COMPLAINTS?

Why it's important: Customers aren't always right. But that doesn't stop them taking their custom elsewhere if you fail to deal adequately with their complaints.

Organisations fight hard to win new customers and then throw them away over a piffling little thing. Years ago I bought a car from a British manufacturer. Within two years it started to rust around the aerial. They refused to repair it under the warranty and I responded by using my influence to stop friends and any organisation I worked for buying their cars. That £200 repair ended up costing them big time. We can calculate the future cash flows (*see Question 69*) from a satisfied customer but we have no idea how costly a dissatisfied customer can be.

Organisations should think of customer complaints not as a source of irritation but as an opportunity to enhance their reputation with customers. This can be achieved by dealing promptly, efficiently and sympathetically with every complaint.

WHAT TO DO

- Train everyone, including yourself, in how to deal with customer complaints, even if the organisation has a specialist complaints team. As a representative of your company you never know when or how a customer might raise a concern.
- Make it easy for the complainant to speak to or see a living, breathing person – without an interminable wait.
- If you must use a call centre, ensure that staff are adequately trained and not just reading off a script. If at all possible locate the centre within the borders of the UK or within whichever country you operate. People don't want to talk to someone on the other side of the world. If you want to benchmark a great phone service take a look at First Direct bank.
- More than anything, customers want to be heard and understood. So listen carefully to what they have to say.
- Acknowledge customers' anger and apologise. Accept their criticism,

stay calm and don't respond to provocation. The criticism isn't personal. You're just the poor sod in the line of fire.

■ Ask questions and clarify any points that are unclear. The more information you have, the better equipped you are to solve the problem.

■ Keep a note of what is said and recap what you've been told, both during and at the end of the conversation. This will reassure the customer that you've understood the problem.

■ Always ask the customer what they want done to resolve the problem. You'll be surprise how often people just want an apology or minor recompense.

■ Complainants want their problem to be solved immediately. Aim to do this, but when further information is required or the matter is passed up the chain explain what's going to happen next and in what timescale. Then deliver on that promise.

■ Keep records of all complaints received. Analyse them monthly and look for any patterns that might indicate a recurring problem. If one is spotted, you need to deal with it at source (*see Question 20*).

■ If you identify a widespread problem, think about going public with it on social networking sites immediately. It's better to reveal the problem than have hundreds of customers complain about you on Twitter or Facebook. But you need to act quickly. *The Times* (4 November 2013) suggested that 69 per cent of 'business crises' spread internationally within 24 hours, while organisations take 21 hours on average to get out their response.

QUESTIONS TO ASK YOURSELF

■ When was the last time that I looked at the customer satisfaction figures? Do I have any figures?

■ What default attitude do I and my staff adopt when a customer complains?

QUESTION 53 WHAT CAN I DO TO IMPROVE THE QUALITY OF MY PRODUCT?

Why it's important: Poor quality costs you money in terms of complaints, returns and lost customers.

As a manager you should constantly strive to improve the quality of the goods or services that you produce.

If you were working in the 1960s or 1970s you would have often heard the phrase 'planned obsolescence'. The idea was that it was bad for the economy to produce goods that lasted too long as this depressed demand and economic growth. For example, it was common for a car to become a moving rust bucket within five years.

Japan led the way out of this cul-de-sac when it adopted the quality philosophy of Edward Deming. Within 15 years 'made in Japan' changed from being synonymous with cheap tat to a sign of good quality, reliable goods.

Quality goods do not have to be expensive. Any item or service that does the job it was designed for and continues to do so for the duration of its life cycle can be described as a quality product. True quality products can surprise you. For example, a while ago I bought a Tissot watch and promised myself that when it needed replacing I'd buy a Rolex. Seventeen years on I'm still waiting to buy that Rolex.

Organisations need to follow the advice of Tom Peters and Robert Waterman, authors of the international bestseller *In Search of Excellence*, if they wish to improve the quality of their product. Depending on your position in the organisation, you may be limited in what you can do. But that is no reason for failing to adopt a quality mindset and implementing as many of the ideas listed below as you can.

WHAT TO DO

- Senior management is often too remote from the action to know what's going on in the market. So it is important that you listen to customers and front-line staff, since new products and processes are more likely to come from these sources than staff in head office.

- Develop a clear simple management structure with as few senior managers or head office staff as possible.

- Identify and eliminate unnecessary bureaucratic practices whenever you come across them (except where you need good bureaucratic practices, such as in wages and salaries). Replace them with pockets of excellence with a clear customer focus.

- Try always to be proactive. Rather than reacting to customer complaints, seek to eradicate problems at source.

- Allow your staff to exercise their discretion within clearly defined boundaries, especially when it comes to dealing with customers.

- Remember that organisations should stick to doing what they do best and improve on it.

- Make it abundantly clear that quality and customer care is everyone's responsibility – not just those in the customer complaints department.

- Publicly commit yourself and your team to securing improvements in quality.

- Train your staff in quality management and genuine customer care.

- Record all complaints and production mistakes and use this information to trace and eradicate recurring problems at source (see Question 20).

QUESTIONS TO ASK YOURSELF

- How much thought do I give to the quality of the goods and services that I and my team produce?

- When was the last time I adopted a suggestion from customers or front-line staff?

QUESTION 54 # HOW CAN I BUILD STRONG RELATIONSHIPS WITH SUPPLIERS?

Why it's important: Without good, reliable suppliers you can't run your business.

You may think that because you are the customer you hold all the power in any relationship with suppliers (both internal and external). But that is seldom the case. Without their supplies your business grinds to a halt. So it's better to think of your relationship with suppliers as one that is mutually beneficial. For that reason you need to expend just as much time and effort on establishing and maintaining good relationships with them as you do looking after your customers.

WHAT TO DO

WHAT YOU CAN EXPECT FROM SUPPLIERS

- Establish quality standards for the goods and services you're buying/ receiving and make it clear that you will not accept anything less. Your product is only as good as its constituent parts.
- By all means be a demanding customer but make sure that your demands are reasonable. Unreasonable demands destroy your relationship with the supplier.
- Visit your suppliers and talk to the people that handle your account. Tell them that you will be honest, frank and open with them and that you expect the same from them. Insist that if something goes wrong with your order you want to know about it ASAP.
- Explain in words of one syllable that you never want to discover that another customer, of similar size/value, enjoys better benefits, prices or services than you.
- Ask the supplier to keep you informed of new products or changes in existing products that might be of interest to you.
- Find a way to make your business more important/significant to the supplier. Perhaps you can offer to pay more quickly than the industry norm, or agree to place fewer but larger orders. Of course, you will want something in return for this because, as Question 55 says, you never give away a bargaining chip for free.
- Don't shy away from conflict – instead sort it out (*see Question 23*).

WHAT YOU CAN DO FOR YOUR SUPPLIERS

- Place orders in good time and don't expect suppliers to drop everything to meet your impossible deadline.
- Pay on time, especially if you are dealing with a small organisation – cash flow is usually crucial to them. Help them, and they'll work harder to keep you satisfied in return.
- If you find a good supplier, be loyal to them. If the opportunity arises to move to a cheaper supplier, give your current supplier a chance to match the newcomer's offer. Why only match and not beat it? Because you've invested time and money in establishing a good relationship. Do you really want to go through all the hassle of that again? Besides, there is always a risk involved in change.
- Recommend your supplier to other business contacts and pass on to them any opportunities that you see. If they're interested in their customers, they'll do the same for you (*see Question 51*).
- Keep the supplier aware of what's going on in your organisation and of any opportunities to bid for work that might arise.
- If your organisation grows, give your suppliers the opportunity to grow with you. Don't just jettison them in the belief that you've outgrown them.

QUESTIONS TO ASK YOURSELF

- Am I over-reliant on one or two big suppliers?
- Am I getting a good deal/service from those suppliers I use regularly?

QUESTION 55 **HOW CAN I BECOME A BETTER NEGOTIATOR AND GET A BETTER DEAL FROM SUPPLIERS AND COLLEAGUES?**

Why it's important: It's not the meek that shall inherit the earth (in this lifetime) but the best negotiators.

A manager's life can seem like one long series of negotiations. Managers have to negotiate with their employers, boss, colleagues, staff, suppliers, customers and stakeholders on a bewildering array of issues. If you're a soft touch, you'll find yourself on the receiving end of some dire negotiations. But if you are too tough then people will be wary of you. Effective negotiators aim for a win/win outcome (*see Question 23*).

For the purpose of this entry I've assumed that the negotiation is between a buyer and supplier. However, the same principles apply in all negotiations.

WHAT TO DO

WHAT TO IDENTIFY BEFORE THE NEGOTIATION STARTS

- What do you want to get out of the negotiation?
- What trades are you willing to make as part of the negotiations and, if possible, what trades do you think the other party might be willing to make?
- Who are the alternative suppliers if agreement can't be reached? (You need to be able to walk away from the negotiation if you have to.)
- What has your past relationship been like with your supplier (if any) and how might that affect the negotiations?
- Who has the most to lose if negotiations fail?
- What compromises would you be willing to accept to make a deal?

HOW TO NEGOTIATE EFFECTIVELY

- Avoid the situation where you are reliant on achieving an agreement. Always have, or at least give the impression you have, other options.
- If you are selling, don't talk about a price until the sale has been agreed in principle. If you do, you'll find yourself under pressure to

concede further ground as negotiations continue. Obviously, if you are buying, try to start price negotiations as soon as possible.

■ Find out what the other person's 'full shopping list' is. Do this before you start negotiating so that you make it difficult for them to add additional items later.

■ Try to engineer the situation so that the other party mentions price first. Knowing their starting point is a valuable advantage.

■ If you are buying, start with a low offer. If selling, start with a high counter-offer. Neither offer should be influenced by the price the other person mentioned, i.e. use the price you had in mind before negotiations started.

■ During negotiations refuse to make any concession without getting something in return.

■ Keep your goal for the negotiations in mind at all times. Don't let the other party chip away at this.

■ Continually look for tradeable concessions that you can offer to the other party. But don't give anything away for free.

■ Keep accurate notes of the meetings and summarise what has been agreed at regular intervals. This will stop the other party from reopening issues that have previously been agreed.

■ Aim to end the negotiation on good terms with the other party. You never know when, or under what conditions, you might meet again.

QUESTIONS TO ASK YOURSELF

■ What's my biggest failing as a negotiator? Am I assertive enough?

■ Do I see negotiations as a competitive sport or am I happy with a win/win result?

KEY MESSAGES TO TAKE FROM THIS SECTION

- Good business is built on good relationships and not on who the last person standing is.
- Recognise that your relationship with both customers and suppliers is based on mutual need.
- Don't exploit either your customers or suppliers. Exploitation may yield a short-term benefit but in the long term it is destructive to good working relations.
- Always aim for a win/win solution in any negotiation or dispute.
- Treat negotiations with colleagues as you would with any external party.
- Listen to your customers and front-line staff – they know what's going on.
- To improve communication within the organisation, keep organisational structures lean and simple, and avoid bureaucracy wherever possible.

SECTION 6

MANAGING OPERATIONAL PLANS AND BUDGETS

It is rare for a man to miss the mark through holding on to the essentials
Confucius, *Analects* 4.23

INTRODUCTION

What role you play in the preparation of the organisation's strategic plan will depend on your position in the organisation and the approach that your organisation takes to planning. At a minimum you will be expected to support and implement the organisation's strategic plan. Even if you only play a very limited role in strategic planning, you will almost certainly find yourself working on and monitoring the operational plan for your unit, section or department. So it's not possible to ignore the planning and budgetary control cycle of your organisation. Indeed, the higher you climb, the more time you will spend on planning the future of your organisation and monitoring budgets.

Broadly speaking, the attitudes of managers to planning can be divided into three categories:

- There are managers who love planning. They prefer it to doing actual work and will often spend an inordinate amount of time trying to collect every last morsel of information and producing hugely detailed plans that are full of spurious accuracy. Their plans are so detailed and dense that they generate more confusion than light.

- Other managers think that it's a waste of time trying to plan for some inherently unknowable future. They spend very little time collecting data and information for their plans. Instead, they prefer to rely on a wish and a prayer. Any plans that they produce provide insufficient guidance for managers and often fail to plan for events which, if not certain to happen, are highly predicable. Such plans aren't worth the paper they're written on.

- Then there are the managers who know that a good plan should provide a map to the future. But it should be a map that may change as market and environmental conditions change. They preach flexibility in how the journey can be made while keeping their eyes firmly on the ultimate destination. Such managers collect enough information to produce a usable plan but recognise that the plan is only an aid to achieving their objectives. By concentrating on the essentials, such managers will more often than not 'hit the mark' to which Confucius refers.

This section provides some guidelines about operational plans and budgets. If you master these principles, you will get the essentials right.

WHAT ROLE AM I EXPECTED TO PLAY IN PLANNING?

Why it's important: To be an effective manager you must be able to influence the planning process and the targets that are set for you.

There are broadly two approaches to planning that organisations can adopt: top down or bottom up.

SUPPORTERS OF THE TOP-DOWN APPROACH:

Believe that the planning process should only involve senior executives and a few professional planners. This means that there is minimum communication between the planning elite and the organisation's managers and other staff. The only contact occurs when the elite requires managers to supply them with specific information.

Expect that once the plan or budget has been completed, it will be accepted without question by managers and staff.

Assume that its implementation will be straightforward.

The top-down approach, or what Igor Ansoff called the modernist approach, is used (at least in part) by many organisations. Although the above description is obviously a stereotype, the two most obvious flaws of the top-down approach are that it assumes that:

- senior executives and planners know more about what is going on in the business than managers and staff;
- the implementation of any plan is a simple and uncontentious task.

SUPPORTERS OF THE BOTTOM-UP APPROACH:
Reject the idea that the senior executives are the best people to be involved in crafting the organisation's plans. They think senior executives are too remote from the action to know what customers think, feel or want.
Suggest that if management wants to develop a plan then they should listen to, and learn from, their customers and front-line staff.
Argue that product innovation and identification of changing trends does not originate with senior executives but comes from those on the front line.
Believe that data should flow up the organisation through middle managers, who summarise and analyse the data before passing it on to senior managers. The role of the planners is then to work with staff and middle managers to develop the organisation's strategic plan.

WHAT TO DO

IN A TOP-DOWN ENVIRONMENT

- Find out the timetable the planners are working to and provide any information they ask for, along with any other information that you think they should take into account. If they don't ask for information, send it anyway. This will improve the quality and quantity of information available to the planners and will offer some protection against poor decision making due to inaccurate or no information.

- Don't for a moment believe that the implementation of an operation plan is without problems. Brief your staff on the content of the plan and outline its implications for the entire team.

- In consultation with your staff, devise an implementation strategy that takes into account workload and existing areas of responsibility.

- Support your staff during the roll-out of the plan.

- Devise an early warning system that will alert you to the need to change the plan because of changes in the internal or external environment.

- Have in place a monitoring system that will highlight any significant variances between plan and actual performance (see Question 29). Run with positive variances and seek to correct negative variances.

- Keep senior management informed of progress.

IN A BOTTOM-UP ENVIRONMENT

■ Use SWOT and PEST analysis to keep tabs on anything that is going on internally and externally that might affect the organisation and your team (*see Question 48*).

■ If a bottom-up approach is used, planners will be coming to you frequently for data and information, which they will use as input to the strategic plan. Promptly provide any information requested but also send any additional information that is relevant and of which they may not be aware.

■ Remain in regular contact with the planning team, even if that's just 'dropping by' with another piece of information or chatting with people over lunch.

■ As the planning cycle progresses, identify any weaknesses in the process and either try to resolve them or let the planners know.

■ Don't be a one-person team when it comes to providing information. Involve your staff early and ask for their opinions on issues. This will create a sense of ownership and will make the implementation process easier.

■ Unless it's confidential, share with staff details of the plan and its implication for the entire team.

■ In consultation with your staff, devise an implementation strategy that takes into account workload and existing areas of responsibility.

■ Support your staff during the roll-out of the plan.

■ Devise an early warning system that will alert you to the need to change the plan because of changes in the internal or external environment.

■ Have in place a monitoring system that will highlight any significant variances between plan and actual performance (*see Question 29*). Run with positive variances and seek to correct negative variances.

■ Keep senior management informed of progress.

QUESTIONS TO ASK YOURSELF

- How would I describe the approach to planning in my organisation?
- Can I use the planning process as an opportunity to get my team and myself noticed by senior management?

QUESTION 57 HOW DO I PREPARE A STRATEGIC PLAN?

Why it's important: If you want to reach 'the top' you need to demonstrate an ability to think strategically and plan accordingly.

The part you play in the preparation of the strategic plan will depend on three factors: 1) Your role in the organisation; 2) Your seniority; and 3) The organisation's approach to planning, i.e. top down or bottom up (*see Question 56*). The following summarises the main stages in the process.

STAGES IN THE PREPARATION OF THE ORGANISATION'S STRATEGIC PLAN:

Review the organisation's vision statement.

Review the organisation's mission statement.

Collect data and use it to inform changes to the mission statement, above, and the organisation's strategic goals, below.

Using the mission statement and the data collected from the data collection exercise, identify the organisation's strategic goals which if achieved will enable the organisation to 'achieve its mission'.

Once the strategic goals have been confirmed, determine what tactics or approach you will adopt to achieve them.

Specify what targets and tasks have to be achieved, and by which divisions, departments and sections, if the strategic goals are to be achieved.

Devise and implement a monitoring and feedback system.

WHAT TO DO

- Start with the organisation's vision statement. This should be written in the future tense; for example, 'Our vision is to be considered the best company in the world by our customers, shareholders, communities and employees'. Unlike a target a vision may be something the organisation is constantly working towards but which it may never achieve. Consider if your vision statement needs changing or amending.

- The organisation's mission statement summarises its goals and values. If the goals are achieved, without compromising the firm's values, the organisation will move closer to its vision. Undertake a critical review of the mission statement and ask whether the goals are still relevant given the changes in the previous year and predicted future changes.

- To identify changes required to your mission statement, above, and to inform your discussions on strategic goals, below, undertake an analysis of the organisation's current and future position using a range of techniques. For example:
  - Benchmark the organisation's key performance indicators against both competitors and other organisations who have a reputation for excellence (for example, for customer care you might look at First Direct Bank or Guinness Storehouse).
  - Use Gap analysis to determine where the organisation currently is, where it wants to be in one to five years' time and how it's going to close that gap.
  - Use SWOT and PEST analysis to identify the internal and external factors that may impinge on the organisation (*see Question 48*).
- From the revised mission statement list the organisation's strategic goals and identify the tactics that will be used to achieve the goals; for example, outsourcing.
- Working with other managers, break the strategic goals down into a series of tasks and targets that can be delegated to divisions, department and sections. These form the basis of the operational plan for these units (*see Question 58*).
- Because staff have played some part in its preparation you should find that there is less resistance to it than if the plan had just been dumped on them.
- Establish a control system to monitor actual performance against planned performance for both the strategic plan and the operational plan (*see Question 29*).

QUESTIONS TO ASK YOURSELF

- What is my organisation's strategic planning cycle?
- How can I increase my involvement in the planning process?

QUESTION 58 HOW DO I PREPARE AN OPERATIONAL PLAN?

Why it's important: As a manager you will be held accountable for delivery of your part of the operational plan. So you need to get it right or you may find yourself committed to the achievement of impossible targets/tasks.

It's very likely that you are or will be responsible for preparing an annual operational plan for your team, section, department or whole organisation. It's important that you do it as accurately as possible because your performance will be judged against how well you deliver the tasks and targets contained in your plan.

The annual operational plan is the vital link between the organisation's strategic plan and annual budget. It takes the organisation's strategic objectives and turns them into a series of tasks and targets that need to be achieved in the following year if the organisation is to progress towards its long-term strategic objectives. It should also form the basis of the organisation's annual budget. In the best-run companies a budget would be no more than a fully priced operational plan.

AN OPERATIONAL PLAN MUST ADDRESS THE FOLLOWING FOUR QUESTIONS:
Where are we now?
Where do we want to be in a year's time?
What do we need to do to get there?
How do we measure our progress along the way?

An operational plan should be drawn up by the manager who has to deliver it. Alas, in some organisations planning is still the remit of a small band of senior managers and professional planners. If you work in such an organisation, draw up your own operational plan and give it to the planners before they start to decide your future. That way you will at least have some chance of influencing their thinking.

WHAT TO DO

- Working with your boss or the planning team, identify which strategic objectives, in whole or part, relate to your team.

- Pull together a small team of staff and take each objective in turn and break it down into a series of deliverables – a list of tasks/targets (TT) which, if accomplished, would help the organisation to achieve its objective (*see Question 29*).

- For each TT specify in clear terms the desired outcome; for example, a reduction of 30 per cent in complaints by customers.

- Set performance standards for each TT; for example, customer satisfaction with the resolution of complaints must exceed 95 per cent.

- Examine what you have committed yourself and your team to and assess if you have the staff and resources required to achieve your TT. If additional resources are required, what are the chances that you'll get them? If it's unlikely, you'll have to revisit your plan and find a different way to achieve your objective.

- Against every TT place a deadline for completion. For long-term TT you will need to set a series of milestones that you can check at monthly or quarterly intervals.

- Monitor your progress against plan using the approach outlined in Question 29.

- Take corrective action as soon as any shortfalls are identified.

- If you can't resolve a problem or you have a positive variance that might be exploited by other sections, report it to senior management.

QUESTIONS TO ASK YOURSELF

- Are the tasks and targets I'm committed to achievable?
- Are my staff committed to the operational plan?

HOW DO I BUILD A VISION FOR MY TEAM?

Why it's important: A good vision can summarise, clarify and unite a team behind a common purpose.

A good vision statement is an idealised description, in summary form, of what the organisation wishes to become. Essentially it highlights the direction of travel that the organisation wants to take. It doesn't have to be achievable. It can be something that the organisation strives to become or do; for example 'Delight all our customers', 'Put a personal computer in every home, running on Microsoft software', or 'Help people live healthier lives by providing fresh, nutritious food at affordable prices'.

In Questions 2 and 25 I emphasised how important it is to be able to rise above the interests of your own team or department and view issues in organisational terms rather than narrow parochial terms. It is essential that a vision for your team fits comfortably into the organisation's overall vision. If it doesn't, you will attract adverse criticism, opposition and ultimately failure – 'you can't fight city hall' and expect to win.

WHAT TO DO

- Obtain a copy of the organisation's vision and mission statements. Some statements can be quiet obtuse so it's useful to discuss what they mean with one or two other managers.

- Obtain a copy of the organisation's strategic plan. If you played a part in preparing the plan, you will know which aspects of it relate to your team/department (*see Question 57*). If the plan was prepared on high without consultation (*see Question 56*) and delivered to you to implement, you'll need to do a bit of analysis to identify what your contribution is expected to be. A chat with your boss might help you identify this.

- Through the delivery of your annual operational plan (*see Question 58*) it's likely that your team will be required to make a number of contributions to the strategy. Summarise these – not as a series of targets but as a description of what you do. You could start by saying 'The purpose of my team is to ...'.

- Over a week spend 10 or 15 minutes every day rewriting this description until you have distilled down the essence of what your team does – it's purpose – into no more than 50 words.

- Use the whole of one team meeting to consider your description of what you do. Create a vision statement that is no more than 20 words in length – shorter if possible. Don't make the final decision at the meeting but leave it for about a week and allow staff to continue making suggestions.

- Hold a short one-off meeting with staff to consider the various statements and choose one that is short, easy to remember and everyone is satisfied with.

QUESTIONS TO ASK YOURSELF

- Can I summarise the vision I have for my team in less than 20 words?
- Is every member of my staff familiar with the vision statements of the organisation and our team?

QUESTION 60 HOW DO I PREPARE A BUDGET IN NORMAL TIMES?

Why it's important: Managers live and die according to how well they exercise budgetary control. But if the budget is wrong in the first place, you're fighting a losing battle.

Normally the role of the manager in budget preparation is limited to completing a budget for each account they are responsible for; for example, photocopying or lighting, etc. The accountant will send each budget holder a schedule which looks something like that shown below, with the last three columns left blank for the manager to complete. Managers will be asked to base their calculations on current prices and to ignore inflation. On receipt of the completed schedule, the accountant will increase each budget head by the expected inflation rate. This ensures that a consistent rate of inflation is used across the organisation.

Cost code	Expense	Last year's actual spend	Current year's budget	Current year's projected final spend	Budget for next year	Notes
040/001	Salaries	110,789	113,600	114,100	134,000	1
040/012	Advertising	21,186	22,900	24,000	26,000	2
040/021	Stationery	13,456	14,000	13,900	15,000	3

WHAT TO DO

- Take each head of account in turn and follow the procedure detailed below.
- Look at the most recent budget report that you received. Compare the actual spend to date with the current year's projected full-year spend. Does the projected spend look reasonable? If so, fine – you can proceed. If not, you need to speak to your accountant.
- Take the projected spend for the year and deduct from it any non-recurring expenses that were present this year but won't be incurred in the next year. In the example below, temporary staff costing £12,000 were employed in 2014 to deal with a short-term increase in workload.

■ Add in any increases in costs that will affect next year that were not incurred this year. In the example below, salaries will increase in 2015 with the appointment of new staff at a cost of £31,900.

Estimated spend for 2014	114,100
Less non-recurring salary costs in 2014	12,000
Add additional salary costs in 2015	31,900
Budget for 2015	134,000

■ This approach is known as incremental budgeting and has the weakness that it assumes that the bulk of the spending is correct, necessary and will continue at current levels. If you suspect that some accounts are bloated while others are starved of funds, you should analyse what the budget was actually spent on. Your accountant will be able to help you with this.

■ Examining each account does take time but it's something that you should do in a rolling programme over the year. This will release savings that you might be able to transfer to other accounts.

■ Many managers ignore the accountant's request not to add in an element for inflation. The accountant knows this. If you have definitely excluded inflation, tell the accountant. You can't afford to see your base budget cut because the accountant thinks you're trying it on.

■ Remember that the accountant consolidates the schedules into a single budget for senior management, who review the budget and decide if any reductions are required.

■ Resist any attempt to reduce your budget by X per cent across the board. Such cuts are like taking a chain saw into brain surgery. Instead, find the savings required by cutting money from those accounts that have a little fat in them or are less essential than others.

QUESTIONS TO ASK YOURSELF

■ Do I know what we spend our budgets on? Do I need to analyse our spending for the current year?

■ Are we getting the best value for money from our suppliers (see Question 55)? Do we need to change suppliers?

HOW DO I PREPARE A BUDGET IN TOUGH TIMES?

Why it's important: Managers are under constant pressure to reduce costs but at the same time improve productivity. The approach outlined here can help you achieve both.

Question 60 explained how budgets are prepared using an incremental approach. This is fine in normal circumstances but when severe reductions in the budget are required it's not enough. What you need to do is adopt a zero-based approach to budgeting. Ignore last year's budget and actual budget spend and instead start with a blank sheet of paper and build your budget from the ground up. Use this approach and you'll save more than 10 per cent – without crippling your operation.

Because I can't possibly know what industry you work in, the examples given below are simple and generic.

WHAT TO DO

- Discuss with your accountant what you intend to do and see what assistance they can give you. If the accountant has any sense they will jump at the offer as it provides them with an insight into how managers prepare a budget and their priorities – information that can be invaluable to them in the future.

- Start by examining the operational plan for your team. If you don't have one, list all the work that your team will be expected to perform in the coming year.

- Create a separate working document, paper or computer-based, for every budget heading that you are responsible for; for example, staffing, materials, stationery, etc.

- Take each budget head in turn and calculate how much you will spend on it. Don't look at last year's figures. Let's take staffing as an example:

  - List each member of staff and the salary they receive, and factor in any pay rises or increments that each person may receive in the next financial year. This becomes your baseline staffing budget.

  - Then consider if you could reduce your staffing levels or reduce the working hours of specific staff without adversely affecting your operation.

- Finally, review the staff turnover figures for your team and calculate how many months you are likely to run short-staffed next year before any vacancy is filled. Be conservative in calculating this figure. Deduct any saving from your baseline figures.

■ Based upon your expected level of activity, estimate how much you are likely to spend on direct costs and overheads (*see Question 67*) and see if you can reduce any heading. Take stationery as an example:

- Consider to what extent stationery can be reduced by using email, texting or social media more creatively.
- Can further savings be made by bulk buying or from using one or two suppliers only?
- Is the quality of the stationery too high – do you really need 100gm paper for general photocopying? Wouldn't 80gm be sufficient?
- The same approach can be applied to most items of expenditure.

■ Follow the same process for materials:

- Start by examining your output targets for next year. If production is going to be down, check that this is reflected in the cost of material and wage/salaries.
- As with stationery, look to bulk-buy materials.
- Consider substituting some or all of the materials for alternatives or reduce the quality of the materials purchased – provided they still meet the specification required.

■ Don't include any hidden contingency funds.

QUESTIONS TO ASK YOURSELF

■ Who on my team can help me analyse the figures?

■ What are the budgets I must protect at all costs?

QUESTION 62   # HOW DO I MONITOR A BUDGET EFFECTIVELY?

Why it's important: A budget/actual report has no value unless a manager uses it to exercise budgetary control.

Accountants don't exercise budgetary control. They may issue the budget/actual report but that's not budgetary control. Budgetary control only occurs when a manager looks at the report, identifies a variance between the budget and actual income or expenditure and takes action either to correct the variance (where it's adverse) or to build on it (where it's positive, for instance when sales exceed forecast).

Typically a budget actual report will be sent to account holders monthly and will look something like this:

Cost code	Budget heading	Budget to 31/7/14	Actual to 31/7/14	Variance £	Favourable/ Unfavourable
044/1007	Copper wire	31,455	32,607	1152	U
044/1008	Extrusion wastage	2,780	2,685	95	F

As a manager you need to know how the budget figure to date has been calculated as this can have an effect on how you interpret the variances. Accountants generally use one of the following methods.

BUDGET CALCULATIONS:

Simple accumulation method: That is where the total budget is divided by 12 and one-twelfth is added to the budget figure as each month passes. This is not much use if you know that most of your sales occur between August and March. Despite this, it remains the most common method used.

Seasonally adjusted: If the organisation's sales are affected by seasonal variations the accountant may take this into account when allocating the budget. For example, a firework manufacturer would expect to see sales increase substantially during late September, October and early November, with smaller increases around Diwali and New Year.

Flexed: This is the least common but perhaps most useful way to show a budget. The accountant amends the budget in line with the level of production/sales. This means that both costs and expenditure will in theory reflect more accurately the actual trading conditions.

WHAT TO DO

- Make sure that you fully understand any budget report that is sent to you. Even if you think you understand it, sit down with your accountant or whoever issues the report and ask them to explain the basis upon which it was prepared and what each figure means.

- Hold a budget actual meeting with those staff who are directly involved in spending the money or achieving the income targets under each budget heading.

- Go through the budget report line by line, and identify the causes of each significant variance.

- Where the variance is unfavourable, explore what you or your team can do to eliminate or ameliorate the problem. Sometimes the problem can't be resolved at your level, for example the rising price of copper on the world markets. In this case all you can do is report the problem up the line and check to see if a favourable balance on another head of account will compensate for the overspend.

- Where the variance is favourable, you want to identify if it's a temporary or permanent phenomenon and look to build upon it.

- Against every variance list the action to be taken, the person responsible and a deadline for completion. This deadline must allow action to be taken and an impact to be made on the figure before the next budgetary control meeting (*see Question 29*).

QUESTIONS TO ASK YOURSELF

- To what extent do I really understand the various reports sent to me by my accountant?

- When was the last time I sat down with my accountant and went through the budget reports and discussed my unmet needs?

KEY MESSAGES TO TAKE FROM THIS SECTION

- Remember that all plans and budgets are best estimates of what the future holds. It's therefore pointless trying to get every tiny detail correct.
- Remember that big organisations are like oil tankers – they require a lot of early actions in order to change their direction or stop them.
- Train yourself to think one, three, and five years ahead.
- Develop your strategic-thinking skills.
- Fight to be involved in the preparation of your operational plan and budget. If you don't, you run the risk of having to implement someone else's unworkable plan or budget.
- Know exactly what your budgets are spent on, and where the scope for reducing spending or increasing income lies.
- Align any vision you have for your team with the organisation's overarching vision.

SECTION 7

UNDERSTANDING FINANCIAL JARGON

Approach your duties with reverence and be trustworthy in what you say; avoid excess in expenditure.
Confucius, *Analects* 1.5

INTRODUCTION

The information in this section is designed to demystify some of the accounting jargon that can often cause non-financial managers confusion. It's intended to provide you with enough information to understand what your accountant is talking about and to ask the right questions. Because I don't expect you to actually apply the information in practice there is no 'What to do' section in any of the entries – except Question 76, which asks the question 'How can I increase the organisation's profits?'

This section has two specific aims:

- To give you an understanding of the key accounting terms that get thrown about as if everyone understands them – because many don't. Without this knowledge you are excluded from the financial conversation and you'll find it difficult to ask the right questions.
- To demonstrate why accounts are not the mathematically accurate statements that many people think they are. To misquote Disraeli, 'There are lies, damn lies and financial accounts'.

I realised the need for a basic outline of key accounting terms and ideas many years ago when I was talking to a chief executive in the public sector whose organisation had just become independent of local government control. It quickly became clear that he did not understand the difference between cash and profit. Which was a bit of a worry as he was running a large autonomous organisation that had to at least break even over a three-year period if it was to survive. But if you think that this financial ignorance is restricted to the public sector, what about the sales manager of a national car franchise who insisted that in his organisation the sales figure was reported in the balance sheet and that 'Garage accounts are different in content and layout to all other organisations'. If only wishing made it so.

If you already have a good understanding of accounting jargon, feel free to skip this section. However, I'll let you into a secret. It was only after I qualified as an accountant that I truly appreciated what an artificial and manmade construct accounting is. I had been too obsessed with just passing the exams to question the rules of the game while I was studying. If the rules are changed, and they can be, the profit reported by all companies can also change. So you might just want to give this section a quick once over.

QUESTION 63

WHAT'S THE DIFFERENCE BETWEEN CASH AND PROFIT?

Why it's important: A surprising number of managers don't understand the crucial difference between cash and profit. Such ignorance can seriously damage a manager's credibility.

Cash is real. It physically exists. You can go to the bank, withdraw your money and hold it in your hands.

Profit does not exist in the physical world. It is a figure calculated by processing an organisation's income and expenditure data in accordance with a range of accounting principles, professional practices, accounting standards and professional judgements. For example:

COMMON ACCOUNTING CONCEPTS:

Accruals: Accounts are not prepared on the basis of the cash you have received or paid out in the financial year. They are based on the accruals concept. This concept requires all income and expenditure that arose during the financial year to be included in that year's accounts, regardless of when the payment (exchange of cash) actually takes place. For example, if you receive a gas bill after the financial year ending on 31/12/2015 for fuel used between 1/10/15 and 31/12/2015 you have to include that bill in your costs for 2015.

Depreciation: When a capital item such as new machinery is purchased its cost is spread over the lifetime of the asset. For example, a machine is purchased and paid for during the financial year ending 31/12/2015 at a cost of £90,000. The machine is a capital item, meaning that the organisation will benefit from its use over a number of years, and not just one year. The asset's life is estimated at three years; therefore one-third of the cost (£30,000) is charged to the organisation's profit and loss account as a depreciation charge in each of the next three years, starting with the accounts ending 31/12/2015 (*see Question 70*). However, the full £90,000 cash would have been deducted from the organisation's bank as soon as the invoice was paid.

Bad debt provision: Provisions come in all shapes and sizes, but the most common is the provision for bad debts. Every organisation has a number of debtors who owe the organisation money. Each year the accountant estimates what percentage of these debts may become bad. This becomes the organisation's bad debt provision and it's treated as a charge against profits in the profit and loss account. Effectively it reduces the reported profit. But it's only an estimate and no money has changed hands.

It is entirely possible to have cash in the bank but make a loss. For example, if an organisation has a large stock of trainers (or any item that is fashion sensitive) and suddenly the market finds a new must-have trainer, it is left with stock that it can't give away. This reduces the value of the closing stock, which increases the cost of sales and the total expenditure charged against sales. The result is that the organisation may have to record a loss for that period – even though its bank balance remains healthy.

It's also possible to have very little cash but make a huge profit. For example, a company's sales may be rocketing and it is busy ploughing money into the purchase of new stock in order to meet demand. However, if it is paying its suppliers every 30 days but it is taking over 50 days to collect money from its debtors then it will quickly run out of cash and end up insolvent because of over-trading (*see Question 64*).

That is why cash is – and always will be – king.

QUESTION 64 # WHAT'S THE DIFFERENCE BETWEEN INSOLVENCY AND BANKRUPTCY?

Why it's important: As with cash and profit, confuse these terms in a discussion and you'll lose credibility.

Insolvency refers to cash. Bankruptcy relates to assets and liabilities.

INSOLVENCY:

Occurs when an organisation has insufficient cash to pay its debts as they fall due.

Can be a temporary affair lasting just a few days or weeks as the organisation waits for a large payment, or it can be an early sign that things are going downhill.

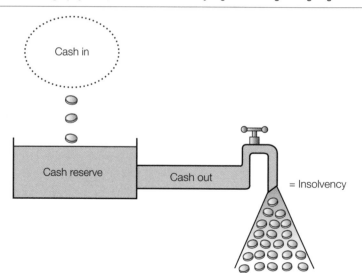

Look out for signs of insolvency; for example, suppliers complaining that they haven't received payment or that payments are unusually late; delays in purchasing essential goods or materials; and, most telling of all, any delays at all in the payment of wages or salaries.

If the signs of insolvency continue for any significant length of time, think about abandoning ship (*see Question 49*).

BANKRUPTCY:

Occurs when an organisation's total liabilities exceed its assets.

Is often terminal, with the organisation entering administration and all its assets being sold to pay off, as far as possible, its creditors.

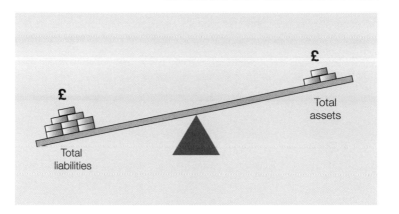

If the organisation enters into bankruptcy you may find yourself out of a job as the administrator seeks to cut costs by letting everyone but essential staff go. It might appear that your best option is to jump ship before you find yourself walking the plank (*see Question 49*).

Alternatively, if you have the bottle, know the business, believe that its failure is down to poor management, is underpinned by a good business model and you can find enough like-minded people within or outside the company and have access to the required capital, you might be interested in making a bid for it. A bankruptcy offers the opportunity to jettison all that was holding the firm back in terms of outmoded ideas, inefficient practices, and disgruntled and unproductive workers. It's an opportunity for those with the courage to seize it.

QUESTION 65 WHAT'S VALUE FOR MONEY?

Why it's important: Every organisation must pursue economy, efficiency and effectiveness if it wants to survive and prosper.

Value for money (VFM) is a concept that came to prominence in the UK in the early 1980s and became one of Margaret Thatcher's foundational strategies to control public sector expenditure. It has since found its way into most organisations in one form or another.

VFM consists of three interrelated concepts:

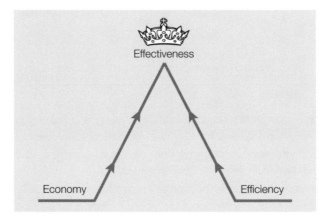

- **Economy** is concerned with obtaining goods of the right standard at the least cost.
- **Efficiency** is concerned with maximising the production of goods and services at the required standard from the least input of resources; for example, an increase in the number of blanks pressed from a one-metre-square sheet of metal represents an increase in efficiency.
- **Effectiveness** is a measure of how successful the organisation has been in achieving its stated objectives.

Of the three concepts, effectiveness is the most important. It's pointless being economic and efficient if the organisation is in pursuit of the wrong objectives or fails to achieve them.

As a manager you can play an active part in ensuring that your operation achieves economy and effectiveness. You can also contribute towards effectiveness: when discussing your targets with your manager (*see Question 8*) or setting targets for yourself or staff (*see Question 29*) always think 'How does this target fit into my operational plan and the organisation's strategic plan?'

QUESTION 66

WHAT'S THE DIFFERENCE BETWEEN A BUDGET AND A FORECAST?

Why it's important: As a manager you are almost certainly going to be responsible for managing a budget.

A budget is used to manage and control an organisation's income and expenditure over a stated period (usually one year). A forecast is a prediction of the organisation's position at some point in the future.

A BUDGET:

If well prepared, should be a costed version of an organisation's operational plan (*see Question 60*). It can be seen as an operational plan with a price ticket on it.

Is prepared internally by the organisation's staff.

Is used to monitor and control the organisation's income, expenditure and investment over a period of one year.

A FINANCIAL FORECAST:

Is a prediction of the organisation's business position at a specified point in the future.

Can be compiled internally by the organisation's staff or externally by a variety of agencies and individuals such as investment analysts, competitors and business commentators.

Uses historic data and future trends to identify the state of the organisation at a specified time in the future, which is often more than one year.

Is not used to monitor or control income or expenditure.

The most difficult part of preparing a financial forecast is predicting future revenue. It is easier to estimate future costs, since there is historical data upon which costs can be estimated with some degree of accuracy. However, as stated previously, the further into the future you try to predict events, the less accurate you will be.

WHAT'S THE DIFFERENCE BETWEEN DIRECT COSTS AND OVERHEADS?

Why it's important: Direct and indirect costs are used to calculate the organisation's gross and net profit.

UNDERSTANDING COSTS:

Direct costs are the costs incurred in the production of the organisation's goods or services. They only include the materials used in the production of the goods or service, and the salaries/wages paid to those people directly involved in the production process.

Overheads are all the other expenses that the organisation incurs as it tries to sell its goods or services. They include such things as advertising, admin salaries, staff training and development, R&D expenses, rental costs, rates, etc. These costs are referred to as indirect costs or overheads.

The organisation's *gross profit* is calculated by deducting the direct costs from sales.

The organisation's *net profit* is calculated by deducting the overheads from the gross profit.

QUESTION 68 WHAT ARE THE DIFFERENCES BETWEEN COST, TRADING AND INVESTMENT CENTRES?

Why it's important: As a manager it is extremely likely that you will have responsibility for one of the above centres.

Cost centres exist in nearly all organisations and you can expect to be responsible for one or two centres. Trading centres are less common, but you may find yourself in charge of one. Investment centres are usually run by a senior executive. You need to know the difference between all three centres and how income and expenditure is coded/allocated to them.

HOW INCOME, EXPENDITURE AND CAPITAL ITEMS ARE CODED AND ALLOCATED TO A PARTICULAR CENTRE:

All income and expenditure is coded to a specific account heading; for example, 01 for salaries.

A cost centre, trading centre or investment centre is usually a division, department, section or team, which is given a code to identify it; for example, 044 for the goods received section.

Using the code 044/01 it's then possible to record the amount of salaries paid to staff in the goods inward section.

BUSINESS CENTRES:

A cost centre is an identifiable area of activity. This might be a department, section, team or even a group of machines to which all the direct and overhead costs (*see Question 67*) are coded/allocated. As cost centre manager you will be required to exercise budgetary control over all or some of the costs charged to that centre. Cost centres are also known as expense centres.

A trading centre is also an identifiable area of activity, such as a division, department or unit. However, unlike a cost centre, it contributes directly to the overall profit of the organisation. It is therefore possible to delegate to it responsibility for a percentage of the organisation's income as well as expenditure. Managers of trading centres are expected to manage the centre's expenditure and also achieve its profit target.

An investment centre is a department or area of operations where the manager is responsible for the control and management of income, expenditure, assets and liabilities. The manager's performance is assessed by calculating the rate of return (*see Question 74*) The rate achieved is compared to past performance, predicted performance and the returns achieved by other investment centres in the organisation over the same period.

QUESTION 69 WHAT IS DISCOUNTED CASH FLOW?

Why it's important: Any manager who makes a capital purchase or long-term investment needs to understand how accountants and banks evaluate such investments.

The value of £100 today is greater than the value of the same £100 in a year's time – inflation will see to that. Therefore when calculating the true return on an investment, be it the purchase of shares or a piece of equipment, it's necessary to take this reduction in value into account. That's what discounted cash flow (DCF) does. It reduces the value of future returns to the net present value (NPV).

For example, say you wish to purchase a machine for £10,000. You've estimated that if purchased it will increase income by £3,000 a year for four years and £1,000 in the fifth year before it has to be replaced. These unadjusted figures are known as future values (FV). The discount rate is set at the predicted inflation rate of 3.5 per cent for each of the next five years.

Descriptor	FV	Discount rate 3.5%	NPV
Year 1 additional income	3,000	100.0	3,000
Year 2	3,000	96.5	2,895
Year 3	3,000	93.0	2,790
Year 4	3,000	89.5	2,685
Year 5	1,000	86.0	860
Total NPV of future additional income			12,230
Purchase price			10,000
NPV of return on capital investment			2,230

On this basis it's worth purchasing the machine because it will increase income by £2,230 over five years. However, if the chosen discount rate proves to be understated the result can be rendered useless. This becomes a real problem when the calculation can extend over 10, 20 or 30 years.

DCF is a valuable tool when evaluating or comparing investments, proposed actions or purchases. Other things being equal, the action or investment that shows the greatest excess of NPV over cost is the best investment/decision.

The discounting rate used may not be the rate of inflation but the minimum rate of return that the organisation has set for all capital investments. This figure will probably be significantly higher than the rate of inflation.

It should be obvious from the above that any DCF calculation contains a number of difficult-to-quantify variables. This has implications for the level of accuracy that can be achieved. Therefore, use DCF to compare the returns on competing projects as indicative of future returns and not as a precise calculation.

WHAT'S THE DIFFERENCE BETWEEN REVENUE EXPENDITURE AND CAPITAL EXPENDITURE?

Why it's important: Revenue and capital items are treated differently in the organisation's accounts.

Expenditure can be divided into two broad areas.

REVENUE AND CAPITAL EXPENDITURE:

Revenue expenditure is the day-to-day expenditure that the organisation incurs as it goes about its business of producing and selling goods and services. Revenue expenses include materials, heating, lighting, admin and management salaries, stationery, photocopying, etc. They are the daily costs of doing business and are charged to the organisation's trading, profit and loss account.

Capital expenditure is incurred when the organisation buys an asset such as a new property, machinery or truck. These items have a benefit that will last many years, and to charge the full cost to the year in which they are purchased would distort the reported profits and make comparison between years difficult. To overcome this, accountants spread the cost of the asset over its lifetime by charging an amount of depreciation each year to the profit and loss account.

There are different ways in which depreciation can be calculated. For example, a machine is purchased for £100,000 and is expected to last five years. What's the yearly depreciation charge?

- **Straight-line depreciation** is the simplest method and involves charging the same amount each year to the profit and loss account over the life of the asset. So:

£100,000 / 5 = a depreciation charge of £20,000 per year.

However, if the accountant thought that the machine would have a second-hand value of £25,000 after five years the calculation could become:

£100,000 − £ 25,000 / 5 = £15,000 per year.

- **The reducing balance method** requires the accountant to decide the rate at which the asset will depreciate. Let's assume that they decide to use 20 per cent per year, in which case the calculation is:

Year	Cost	Balance	Depreciation @ 20%	Asset value
1	100,000		20,000	80,000
2		80,000	16,000	64,000
3		64,000	12,800	51,200
4		51,200	10,240	40,960
5		40,960	8,192	32,768

It's the accountant's choice as to which method to use. But since the method used will change the amount of profit reported whichever method is adopted must be applied consistently in future years.

Increasingly 'small' assets, such as computers and office fixtures, fittings and furniture, are written off in the year in which they are purchased. But again, if this policy is adopted, it must be applied consistently.

QUESTION 71 # WHAT'S THE DIFFERENCE BETWEEN FIXED AND VARIABLE COSTS?

Why it's important: An understanding of fixed and variable costs enables you to calculate the breakeven point.

Costs can be classified in various ways. In Question 67 costs were analysed into direct costs and overheads. These same costs can be described as either fixed or variable costs.

■ **Fixed costs** are those that remain the same, regardless of the level of production. For example, just because production goes up from 100,000 to 102,000 units doesn't mean an increase in administrative salaries, rates, office heating and lighting, advertising or auditors' fees, and nor would you have to buy a new machine or property to cope with such a change.

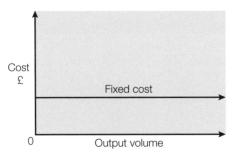

■ **Variable costs** do increase in line with the level of production and include such costs as raw materials, components, packaging or the power used in the manufacturing process, etc.

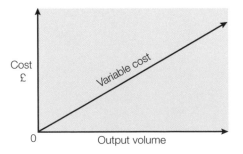

■ **Semi-fixed costs** are those that remain fixed over a range of production levels. For example, it may be possible to manufacture up to 109,999 units with the existing machinery, but if you wanted to push production past 110,000 units you will have to buy a new machine as machine capacity has been reached.

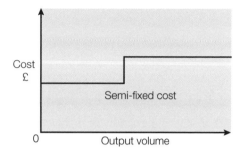

QUESTION 72 WHAT IS BREAKEVEN ANALYSIS AND WHY IS IT IMPORTANT?

Why it's important: Once an organisation reaches breakeven point the profit per unit produced increases significantly as all fixed costs have been recovered and further sales only have to recover the variable costs associated with production.

To break even, every organisation has to recover both its fixed costs and variable costs. For example, an organisation manufactures just one product, which it sells for £20. The variable cost per unit is £10 and fixed costs are £100,000. What's the breakeven point?

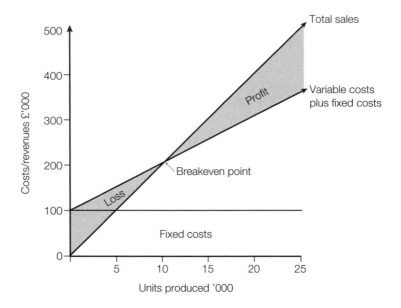

Once the breakeven point is reached, each unit sold generates £10 clear profit:

Sales price £20 – Variable costs £10 = Profit £10

This is because all the fixed costs have been recovered. This leaves management free to decide if they wish to reduce the price of the product temporarily, as a strategy to increase sales further and/or win new customers, or leave the price as it is and enjoy a £10 contribution to profit on each item sold.

HOW DO I CALCULATE A SALES PRICE?

Why it's important: Managers must recognise that they do not calculate sales prices – the interaction of supply and demand does that.

This is a trick question, but one that I have been asked many times during my career. So let me make it clear: *The cost of an item plays no part in the setting of a sales price.*

A sales price is determined by the interaction of supply and demand in the marketplace. Just because an item costs £200 to make does not mean that anyone will be willing to pay £250 for it. Similarly, a comic that cost less than 5 cents to print can sell for $1 million – just as *Amazing Fantasy 15* (marking the first appearance of Spiderman in 1963) did recently.

The only role that a product's cost should play in pricing is deciding if you can afford to compete in the market. If your costs are below the market price, you may decide to play. But before you do so you'll need to decide if you could achieve a better return if you were to invest your resources in a different product.

Set your sales price using the full cost of the item (fixed and variable costs) as there is no guarantee that a new product will achieve breakeven. Once breakeven has been reached (*see Question 72*) you can decide, with the help of your accountant, if the price should be reduced or not.

QUESTION 74 # WHAT ARE THE FOUR MOST USEFUL FINANCIAL RATIOS?

Why it's important: Ratios summarise and highlight essential information in a single figure. But you need to know how to read them.

There are literally hundreds of financial ratios that you can use to assess the financial well-being of any organisation. Some are easy to calculate but others are fairly obtuse and you'd need an accounting qualification to appreciate their full significance. So I've tried to cut through the mass of figures and provide you with four key ratios that taken together cover the main areas of business.

CALCULATING KEY RATIOS:

Profitability: Net profit after tax / Sales × 100
The resulting percentage shows the overall profitability of the organisation and can be compared to the results of other companies in the same sector.

Liquidity: Current assets less stock / Current liabilities
The resulting ratio shows to what extent the organisation's current assets (cash and near cash items) can cover its current liabilities. In previous years a ratio of 1 to 1.5 would have been considered good. Today a figure nearer 1 to 1.1 is considered reasonable. Anything less than 1 means that the organisation may face some problems paying its debts on time, should there be any problems in recovering money from its debtors (*see Question 64*).

Use of assets: Sales / Fixed assets
The resulting ratio shows how many pounds' worth of sales are generated by each pound of fixed assets. It shows how effectively the organisation is using its fixed assets – the higher the figure, the better.

Company performance: Return on capital employed = Profit before tax, interest and dividend / Total capital employed
Total capital employed is defined as total assets less current liabilities (loans and creditors). This ratio gives a broad view of the organisation's overall performance and is a rough equivalent of the rate of return you see on any investment.

The four ratios outlined above will enable you to monitor the basic financial health of your organisation. I suggest that you compile them quarterly and look for trends in the data. They can provide an early warning of both growth and contraction in the organisation.

If you're employed by a public limited company the data will be freely available online. Ask your accountant for help if you have difficulty calculating the ratios. If you work for a private company, partnership or sole trader you may or may not have access to the data required to calculate the ratios.

QUESTION 75 WHAT IS COST BENEFIT ANALYSIS?

Why it's important: It is essential that you take into account factors that are difficult to quantify in financial terms when making decisions.

US Secretary of Defense Robert McNamara developed his fallacy theory during the Vietnam War as a way of explaining why for much of the war America thought it was winning. American reports highlighted measurable information, such as the number of Viet Cong killed or captured and weapon stores destroyed. But they failed to take into account such unquantifiable factors as enemy morale and the desire of the Vietnamese to be free of foreign interference in their country. McNamara's theory consists of four statements. I've adapted it to reflect the needs of managers.

MANAGERS:
Measure what they can easily measure.
Ignore or inaccurately quantify what is difficult to measure.
Assume that if something can't be accurately measured it isn't important.
Assume that what can't be measured doesn't exist.

This means that managers often fail to take into account important data because it is difficult to express in financial terms. Cost benefit analysis (CBA) seeks to address this by allocating a financial value to all costs and benefits. However, CBA lacks methodological rigour/clarity. This means that many CBA exercises suffer from poor quantification of non-financial costs and benefits.

CBA is seldom used in the private sector, where discounted cash flow remains considerably more popular. However, it has been used to calculate such intangible assets as brand value and corporate image.

Where private sector organisations can become involved with CBA is when they enter into contracts with national or local government. For example, CBA has been used to justify the £42 billion cost of the High Speed 2 rail project (HS2). Much of the controversy surrounding HS2 is because it is not clear how the alleged costs and benefits of the project have been calculated. There is a widespread belief that because there are few rules about how costs and benefits are calculated it is possible for accountants and economists to manipulate the figures to provide the answers required to support the project sponsors' position.

QUESTION 76 # HOW CAN I INCREASE THE ORGANISATION'S PROFITS?

Why it's important: No commercial business can survive unless it makes sufficient profit to pay its debts, invest in the future and reward its owners.

If I had a foolproof plan for increasing an organisation's profit I wouldn't be writing this book. I'd be challenging Bill Gates as the richest man in the world. But what I can do is outline a range of strategies that have helped different organisations at different times in their life cycle to increase their profits.

WHAT TO DO

FIRST STEPS

- Establish what the organisation's current income and expenditure is and analyse both into monthly and yearly figures. Involve your accountant if necessary.

- From the numbers above, determine your current profit (which is your total income minus your total expenses within a particular timeframe). What is your net profit percentage now (*see Question 74*)? What do you want it to be in six months? In a year? In five years? Set some goals.

- Make a list of all the sources of income you have and show the amount received against each for the last year split into months. Do the same for expenditure.

EXPENDITURE

- Examine your list of expenditure and ask the most fundamental question of all: 'Do we really need to buy this item?' You'll be surprised how often the answer is no. If you really need the item, continue interrogating the expense and the people who ordered the item. For example, ask 'Why are we spending this amount of money on this item?', 'What benefit does it give us?', 'Could we substitute a cheaper alternative without loss of quality?', 'Can we get a better deal from our suppliers?', 'If we buy in bulk or offer to pay in cash or within 28 days, can we get a discount?' Basically ask any questions that might help you reduce the cost.

- Reduce interest payments by paying off debts that you can afford to clear, or find cheaper refinancing deals.
- Eliminate waste from all aspects of the business.
- Improve economy by purchasing the required goods and materials, of the right standard, at the cheapest rate (see Question 65).
- Increase efficiency and look to increase the amount of output you get from the existing level of inputs (see Question 65).
- Consider sub-contracting some services if it's cheaper; for example, cleaning, IT services, etc.
- Can labour costs be reduced using new technology, part-time or contract staff?

INCOME
- Can you increase selling prices, offer discounts or special deals, and so increase sales?
- Using the Pareto principle, identify the 20 per cent of products that generate 80 per cent of your sales. Can sales of these products be increased to existing customers or new customers attracted?
- Ensure that all invoices are raised on the day of dispatch and that funds are collected within the agreed period of credit. Don't finance other people's businesses. Get the money in and use it to reduce your lending and/or increase the money you can place on deposit or invest in other assets.
- Identify which 20 per cent of customers contribute 80 per cent of your income. What other products do you produce that they might be interested in?
- Identify which 20 per cent of customers cause you the most problems. Then consider, should you ditch them and use the resources saved to win more valuable customers? I've done this and it can be surprisingly effective (although you might get into a row with the sales manager).
- Brainstorm ideas about new products or changes to existing products that might find a market with existing and new customers.
- Get the sales and marketing teams together and brainstorm some cheap marketing and sales promotion ideas. Pinch ideas from customers, supplier, competitors, TV shows and anywhere else you can find a good idea.
- Consider what new markets you can break into at little cost.

- Trial-run some of the ideas and ditch those that don't show a positive return.

- See if there are any complementary services that you can offer your customers. For example, if you are a retail car showroom, do you offer scratch repairs to your customers? Many customers don't repair scratches because they are told that a re-spray is required, but there are plenty of organisations that specialise in just repairing the scratch.

ASSETS

- Examine the assets that your organisation has. Are you maximising your use of them? For example, a few years ago an enterprising zoo was looking at the problem caused by animal waste. One bright spark suggested that instead of disposing of it they should market it as zoo manure. Today many zoos do the same. Continually review your costs, income and asset utilisation rather than tackling one-off events prompted by a current crisis.

- Are you carrying too much stock? Could you reduce stock levels and invest the cash released in paying off loans or investing in new money-making projects? Are there any buildings, machines or land that you don't need which could be sold off or sub-let, and the revenue received invested or placed on deposit? It is sensible to invest in new equipment and processes if it can be shown that in the medium term such investment will increase cash flows and profit (*see Question 69*).

- Are existing fixed assets, such as machinery, costing too much in terms of repair and maintenance? Do you need to replace them with something that is more efficient?

- Improve how you deal with debtors. Stop salespeople selling to anyone with a poor credit record. Improve all credit control procedures, especially chasing bad and doubtful debts. Use a collection agency if necessary.

- Sell off old and obsolete stock for whatever you can get for it. It's taking up room and dropping in value if it is just sitting in your storeroom.

QUESTIONS TO ASK YOURSELF

- Do I see increasing profits as part of my job? If not, why not?
- Have I ever asked my team how we could increase our profits? If not, why not?

KEY MESSAGES TO TAKE FROM THIS SECTION

- The higher you climb, the more important it is that you have a good understanding of accounting terminology.
- A little knowledge is a dangerous thing. The information given in this section is only intended as a taster. Always discuss your accounting or financial information needs with your accountant before you make any financial decision.
- If you find yourself in a financial discussion, don't be afraid to ask 'What do you mean by that?' Asking for clarification when you don't understand something is a sign of intelligence. Pretending to understand something when you don't is just plain stupid.
- Remember that accounts are not the mathematically precise documents that they appear to be.
- Many accountants are frustrated by people's reluctance to seek their advice. Most will be only too happy to help if you ask.
- Prices are set by the interaction of supply and demand in the market – not the cost of producing a product or service.
- There are opportunities in every organisation to increase profits, provided you seek them out.

CONCLUSION

If you read this book in a couple of sittings you may be feeling slightly overwhelmed by the number of problems that a manager can face. Don't be. The questions discussed are those faced by a manager over the course of their career. You'd be very unlucky indeed to find them all landing on your desk at once, or even within a year.

You also need to remember that there is no such thing as the perfect manager – although I have met one or two who thought they were. Such people usually have very little insight into their own strengths and weaknesses and – as Winston Churchill (among others) described them – 'They are [usually] not fit to manage a whelk stall'.

To become the best manager you can be, you have to be true to yourself, your beliefs and attitudes. By all means use the ideas contained in books to inform your practice and don't be afraid to copy examples of best practice that you come across at work. But don't try to be anyone's clone. Create the manager only you can be. A creation that will have strengths and weaknesses. A creation that is a genuine reflection of your personality. A creation that people will recognise as genuine, and therefore come to trust and follow.

FURTHER READING

BOOKS

Adair, J. (2011) *100 Greatest Ideas for Being a Brilliant Manager*. Chichester: Capstone.

Carnegie, D. (2006) *How to Win Friends and Influence People* (new edn). London: Vermilion.

Crainer, S. and Dearlove, D. (2004) *The Financial Times Handbook of Management: The State of the Art* (3rd edn). Harlow: Pearson Education.

Deming, E. (2000) *Out of the Crisis*. Cambridge Mass: MIT.

Drucker, P.F. (2007) *The Essential Drucker*. Oxford: Butterworth-Heinemann.

Greene, R. (2000) *The 48 Laws of Power*. London: Penguin.

Handy, C. (1993) *Understanding Organizations*. London: Penguin.

Hayek, F.A. (2007) *The Road to Serfdom*. Chicago: University of Chicago Press.

Machiavelli, N. (2004) *The Prince* (trans. Bull, G.). London: Penguin.

McGrath, J. and Bates, B. (2013) *The Little Book of Big Management Theories*. Harlow: Pearson Education.

McGregor, D. (2006) *The Human Side of Enterprise: Annotated edition*. New York: McGraw-Hill.

Moss Kanter, R. (1989) *The Change Masters*. London: UnwinHyman.

Mott, G. (2012) *Accounting for Non Accountants* (8th edn). London: Kogan Page.

Northouse, P.G. (2012) *Leadership Theory and Practice* (6th edn). London: Sage.

Townsend, R. (1970) *Up the Organization*. London: Coronet Books.

Townsend, R. (1984) *Further Up the Organization*. London: Michael Joseph Ltd.

Walsh, C. (2008) *Key Management Ratios*. London: FT Prentice Hall.

Wyatt, S. (2010) *The Secret Laws of Management*. London: Headline Publishers.

If you can't find one of the above texts in a bookshop or on Amazon, try www.abebooks.co.uk

JOURNALS

Director
Harvard Business Review
International Journal of Applied Management
Journal of Leadership Studies
McKinsey Quarterly
Management Today
My Business
People Management
Professional Manager

WEBSITES

www.businessballs.com
www.dictionary.com
www.ehow.com
www.entrepreneur.com
www.mindtools.com

Check out the free lectures and materials that are available on the Internet from the world's best universities such as Harvard, Princeton, MIT, Oxford and Cambridge. The American universities in particular are very generous in what they make available to the public.

INDEX